A Narrative of
Colonel Ethan Allen's Captivity

ALSO AVAILABLE FROM THE COPLEY SERIES

Emergent Texts in American Literature
Stephen Carl Arch, *Series Editor*

*Running a Thousand Miles for Freedom,
Or, The Escape of William and Ellen Craft from Slavery*
Edited by John Ernest

T.S. Arthur's
Ten Nights in a Bar-Room
Edited by Jon Miller

Paul Dunbar's
The Fanatics
Edited by Lisa Long

Mary Wilkins Freeman's
Pembroke
Edited by Mary Rigsby

Anna Cora Mowatt's
Mimic Life
Edited by Jeffrey Richards

Susanna Haswell Rowson's
Slaves in Algiers
Edited by Jennifer Margulis and Karen Poremski

Emergent Texts in American Literature

A Narrative of
Colonel Ethan Allen's Captivity

Edited by
Stephen Carl Arch
Michigan State University

A COPLEY EDITION

ISBN: 978-1-58390-009-3

Library of Congress Catalog Number: 99-074753

Cover image: *Allen in the Provost Prison.* 1858. Photograph.
https://www.loc.gov/item/2004674893/.

530 Great Road
Acton, MA 01720
www.xanedu.com

Contents

Introduction

Long before he died in 1789, Ethan Allen had become a mythical figure, thanks in large measure to his own inclination for self-aggrandizement. For many of his followers and, later, for many Americans, he was a larger-than-life western hero, tough, swaggering, democratic, and brave. Though it began during his own lifetime, this mythologizing continued long after Allen's death and well into the nineteenth century, as novelists, biographers, and historians "tailored [Allen] to fit the mantle of a founding father" (McWilliams 258). It has been impossible for twentieth-century biographers of Allen entirely to dispel the myths that grew up around him, because "Contemporary records provide no answer to the most significant questions of Allen's life" (264). We do not know, for example, why Allen was never called to active service in the Continental Army, what words he actually spoke to the commander at Fort Ticonderoga as he requested its surrender in 1775, or whether he really wrote all or part of the Deist tract *Reason the Only Oracle of Man*, which he published under his own name in 1784. Myths persist because we find them socially or culturally or politically useful, of course, but they also persist because more plausible and evidently true stories are not recoverable.

We do know that Ethan Allen was born in 1738 in Litchfield, Connecticut, near the western frontier of that colony. His father was a farmer with an eye toward buying land, a trait that most of his six sons imitated. Ethan, the oldest, showed an early inclination for learning, despite the fact that the frontier towns his family inhabited had no schools. At the age of seventeen, he was sent to the town of Salisbury, Connecticut, to study with a minister in preparation to enter Yale College. But the unexpected death of his father soon brought the young man back to the family farm, where he took over the role of father to his seven siblings. He would always regret his lack of a college education.

In 1757, during the Seven Years' War between England and France, Allen briefly enrolled in a military campaign against the French, but his company disbanded before it saw action. He was not and never would be a trained military man, as his actions in the American Revolution later proved. Allen married, purchased land in Connecticut, and began to raise his own family. Until 1770, he struggled to lift his extended family into prominence: he bought and sold land ("speculating," this was called), started several businesses, and tried as best he could to educate himself. An itinerant, self-educated doctor named Thomas Young led Allen to repudiate his Calvinist upbringing in those years; later in life, Allen published *Reason the Only Oracle of Man* to express what he had learned from and with Young. Meanwhile, however, Allen had little success in becoming a wealthy landowner, and his lower social status played a large role in his attempt to remake himself, both through land deals and through stories of his physical and intellectual prowess.

In 1770, as part of his land speculation deals, Allen purchased three lots in the New Hampshire Grants, an area of land between New York and New Hampshire. It was a fateful purchase. Boundaries between colonies, especially in the west on land uninhabited by whites, were vague and imprecise in the eighteenth century. Both colonies claimed the right to develop the Grants. After twenty years of wrangling, the dispute had been "settled" by King George III in the mid-1760s; he ruled that New York had undisputed right to the land. But years of land grants by New Hampshire—including the lots that Allen purchased—led to the area actually being settled by people from New England, not New York. When New York tried to enforce the king's decision in the late 1760s and early 1770s, its officials discovered that those settlers were not willing to move or to have their land re-granted to them by New York. Resistance became armed when the angry settlers found a leader who could organize them and direct a campaign to make the region independent: Ethan Allen. More than a thousand men, at one time or another, joined his Green Mountain Boys in resistance to New York.

That resistance took two main forms, physical intimidation and propagandistic pamphleteering, and Allen excelled at both. A physically intimidating and apparently charismatic man, Allen enjoyed confronting New York's lawyers, judges, and surveyors when they ventured into his territory, threatening them with violence and subjecting them to verbal insults. Few of them dared to stand up to Allen alone, much less to the hardy frontiersmen who stood alongside him. In published pamphlets, Allen attacked New York and its laws, hammering home in vociferous prose his claim that New York's grasping aristocrats were tyrants bent on appropriating land lawfully cleared by hard-working settlers. "The Government of New York," Allen spit in one pamphlet published in 1775, appointed "Pests of society to the Rank of Magistrates" in the contested territory, evincing thereby its "premeditated Harmony of Design" to divide and conquer the region and then give it to grasping "sordid Wretches," "Land Monopolizers from New York," whose only interest was in depriving hard-working farmers of their recently cleared acreage. Even without a college education, Allen grasped the potential usefulness of printed texts in the larger urban centers and colonial capitals of New England, and he took ample advantage of the printing press as a tool of propaganda.

The area that the Green Mountain Boys defended in the early 1770s did not become a state until 1791. Indeed, for a brief moment in 1781, annoyed with Congress's refusal to admit Vermont to the union as the fourteenth state, Allen toyed with the idea of returning Vermont to the British Empire. The political jockeying that took place in the 1780s, much of it with Allen at its center until his death in 1789, is beyond the scope of this introduction. But it should be noted that Allen calls attention to Vermont's awkward status at the end of his *Narrative*: upon his return from captivity in 1778, he notes, fourteen cannon were discharged in Bennington, Vermont, "thirteen for the United States, and one for young Vermont." Vermont had produced a written Declaration of Independence, modeled on Jefferson's, in 1777; it had, under Allen's leadership, taken Fort Ticonderoga from the British in 1775, in the first offensive operation against the British; and it had tied its attempt to free itself from the "tyranny" of New York and its royal governor, William Tryon, to the thirteen colonies' attempt to free themselves from Great Britain and its king, George III. Still, as the historian Michael Bellesiles writes, "Vermont stood separate and alone. Its military service had not won it political legitimacy. Congress, it appeared, had betrayed Vermont's people in the face of their heroism"

(148). It is no wonder that Allen had his *Narrative* printed in Philadelphia in 1779: he wanted to make sure that America's political leaders knew of his and Vermont's role, long-suffering and patient, in the American Revolution.

Allen's *Narrative* is itself, then, a political pamphlet, one that was reprinted eight times in 1779 and 1780. It was very popular. Allen wrote it in the context of the literature he knew, and that included the genre we now refer to as the captivity narrative, in which (traditionally) a white captive told of his or her captivity at the hands of Indian captors. The literary critic Daniel Williams has astutely read Allen's *Narrative* as a "captivity narrative [that] reflected the conventions of [these] earlier Indian captivity narratives" (331). Redemption or freedom for Allen comes to mean liberty, not the conversion to a truer or renewed or more heartfelt Christianity that it meant in many of the early captivity narratives. Through his trials and torments, Williams argues, Allen teaches his readers "that submission to tyranny resulted in a death of one sort or another, that happiness depended on liberty, and that liberty demanded total commitment" (340). Allen's lesson, Williams concludes, was a self-conscious representation—an "artistic process of self-creation" (341)—in which Allen remade himself into the person he wanted to be: an honorable gentleman whose motives were pure and disinterested and self-evident.

We know for sure that Allen was taken captive by the British in September 1775 as he tried in an ill-conceived attack to take Montreal from the British. He had no commission from the Continental Congress or from a colonial government ("though," he says, the officers commissioned by Congress "engaged . . . that I should be considered as an officer the same as though I had a commission"), which created problems both for the British who captured him and for Allen himself in captivity. He was finally exchanged for a British colonel in May 1778. Throughout his narrative of these two and a half years, Allen is careful to describe the cruel treatment he received at the hands of his British captors. Writing in late 1778 and early 1779, Allen was trying both to exercise literary revenge on the British and to reinvigorate the revolutionary cause, which was flagging because the American people had lost their initial enthusiasm for a war that had already dragged on for four long years.

So, for example, on board the British ship *Mercury* en route to Halifax in 1776, Allen found himself under a cruel captain named Montague, who "was loaded with prejudice against every body; and every thing that was not stamped with royalty." Montague "seemed to think," Allen says, "that heaven and earth were made merely to gratify the king and his creatures," and as a result he denies his American prisoners food and medical assistance. The entire British prison system, Allen remarks bitterly near the end of the narrative, may "with propriety [be] called the British inquisition," directed by "the British council" and "perpetrated" in America by "monster[s]" like William Howe, Joshua Loring, and John Burgoyne. Allen describes in detail wretched conditions on prison ships and in the makeshift New York prisons, focusing on the brutal punishments, rotten food, unsanitary floors and bedding, lack of medical attention, and epidemics. Captivity in his account is truly and sensibly horrifying. He clearly wants his contemporary readers to feel the realities of captivity. Thinking about them is not enough: Americans had to *feel* what the captives felt.

Daniel Williams has rightly argued that the Indian captivity narrative was an important shaping influence on Allen's account of his captivity. Now, the Indian captivity narrative tended to represent a binary opposition between "us and them," between darkness and light, savagery and civilization, demons and saints. Mary Rowlandson, in her 1682 captivity narrative, for example, describes her Indian captors as "wolves," "hell-hounds," and "devils," whereas the white colonists are "sheep" and children of God. We might expect, then, given Allen's characterization of the British prison system as an "inquisition," that the binary system at work in his narrative would be American versus British. All Americans should be good; their enemies should be evil. Yet Allen often meets with a "generous enemy." "One of the officers [on one of the prison ships], by the name of Bradley, was very generous to me, he would often send me victuals from his own table." "My personal treatment by lieutenant Hamilton, who commanded [Pendennis] castle, was very generous." "The guard which was set over us [in Halifax], was . . . touched with the feelings of compassion." The British as Allen presents them are not in and of themselves demonic or monstrous.

Nor are the Americans entirely sanctified in liberty. One guard over Allen in New York "was composed of tories from Connecticut. . . . They

were very full of their invectives against the country, swaggered of
their loyalty to their king, and exclaimed bitterly against the 'cowardly
yankees.'" American Tories watch with "delight and triumph" as
prisoners from the Continental Army die in crowded churches in
New York. "I have observed the British soldiers to be full of their
blackguard jokes," Allen writes, "and vaunting on those occasions,
but they appeared to me less malignant than tories." The American
Tories figure as do Howe and Burgoyne, as "monsters" perverted in
their designs.

Allen does figure the conflict in his *Narrative* in binary terms, even
if those terms are not "American" and "British." Critics have noted
how Allen divides the men he encounters into those who recognize
him as a gentleman and those who do not. "Early in his life," Daniel
Williams tells us, "Allen had claimed for himself gentleman-status,
and now, during his captivity, his greatest struggle was to maintain
this status in the most abject circumstances" (334). I am not sure that
a reading of either the biographies of Allen or of Allen's *Narrative*
itself warrants an assertion that Allen claimed "early in his life" the
status of a gentleman, but he does claim it in the *Narrative* when he is
fighting for the revolutionary cause. This desire to be seen as a gentleman is, in fact, where Williams finds Allen "remaking" himself.
Born on the frontier in western Connecticut, lacking any sort of formal
education, and isolated by the rigors of frontier existence, Allen proclaimed himself a gentleman in his *Narrative*, demonstrating in the
process what Williams calls "his power of self-creation" (341).

In one incident, for example, while held at Pendennis Castle,
Allen is paraded in front of "numbers of gentlemen and ladies"; he
asks one "gentleman for a bowl of punch, and [the gentleman]
ordered his servant to bring it, which he did, and offered it me, but I
refused to take it from the hand of his servant; he then gave it to me
with his own hand," and Allen drinks it down. A gentleman himself,
Allen will accept the drink only from the hand of another gentleman,
not a servant. Elsewhere, Allen is often treated as a private soldier,
housed with the other privates, denied the luxuries normally
afforded to commissioned officers, and told explicitly that he is not a
"gentleman." Many of the British commanders, Allen sighs, "knew
not how to behave towards a gentleman of the military establishment." But, in defense of the British military, Allen had no commission

from a colonial government or from the Continental Congress—not that the British recognized such commissions in the early years of the war—nor did he "appear" to be a gentleman. He swears grievously, dresses barbarously, acts (by his own admission) like "the madman," and "swagger[s] over those who abused" him. In England, two clergymen come to see him and are surprised that Allen "should understand a syllogism or regular mood of argumentation. . . . To see a gentleman in England [argue thus], regularly dressed and well behaved, would be no sight at all; but such a rebel, as they were pleased to call me, it is probable was never before seen in England." Allen looks and acts like a rough frontiersman, not a member of the gentry.

Many people do, however, recognize Allen as a "gentleman" and treat him accordingly. Sailing from Halifax to New York, Captain Smith of the *Lark* met Allen on the quarter deck and "assured me that I should be treated as a gentleman." Allen tells Smith that he can probably never repay such generosity: "Capt. Smith replied, that he had no reward in view, but only treated me as a gentleman ought to be treated." At Pendennis Castle, Lieutenant Hamilton sends Allen a few marks of gentlemanly status: "fine breakfast and dinner from his own table, and a bottle of good wine." Held on a prison ship in Cork, Allen is given food, clothes, and money by some "gentleman of Cork determined to make my sea stores equal to the Captain [of the ship]." From a "large acquaintance with gentlemen of [Ireland]," Allen says, he can tell the nation abounds in "liberality and bravery." Some people are able intuitively to penetrate Allen's frontiersman's clothes and his rough behavior and see behind them his internal gentlemanly merit.

Allen's definition of a gentleman can be derived from the incidents of his *Narrative*. It involves, first, a sense of honor and a concomitant self-consciousness that honor has a public dimension—in other words, reputation. Musing on the possibility that he might die in prison, Allen reasons that the "cause I was engaged in" was a "worthy" one, worth dying for if need be, and that if he should die he would "be as well treated as other gentlemen of my merit" in the world of spirits. He resolves not to show fear in the face of death so that he "might exhibit a good sample of American fortitude" and so that his "last act [will not be] despicable to my enemies, and [hence will not] eclipse the other actions of my life." Here and elsewhere, Allen is intensely aware of the way his actions will be perceived by others. He is a "sight," as the two clergymen suggest, someone whose behavior is assessed not just for what it says about himself but also for what it says about other things: liberty, gentlemanliness, America, American identity. Later, for example, when some prisoners approach Allen to help them overthrow Captain Smith of the *Lark*—the same Captain Smith who was willing to treat Allen as a gentleman—Allen tells them "that they might depend on it, upon my honor, that I would faithfully guard Captain Smith's life," thereby indeed repaying Smith's initial gentlemanly generosity. The enemy is not the British: it is anyone who fails to understand that society functions smoothly only when honorable men display their honorable intentions. The revolution itself, Allen implicitly reminds his reader at the outset of his *Narrative*, was caused by the "systematical" attempt of Great Britain "to enslave America"—that is, to deprive American subjects of their innate equality to British subjects. British soldiers are not the enemy because they are British; they are the enemy because they (some of them, at least) seek to subjugate their fellow countrymen, their political and social equals in the eyes of Allen.

For the British, of course, honor is class-based; many British officers cannot see Allen as honorable because he is not of noble birth or superior social position. Allen knows this: in his "Introduction" he asks his audience "to excuse any inaccuracies . . . as the author has unfortunately missed a liberal education," one of the signs of gentle breeding for men in the eighteenth century. But his bid in the *Narrative* is to shift the definition of gentlemanliness from heredity and training to individual, innate merit. In this, his bid is similar to Jefferson's repeated attempts (beginning in 1779) in Virginia and the United States to make education available to all "those persons . . . whom nature hath endowed with genius and virtue . . . without regard to wealth, birth or other accidental condition or circumstance," as he wrote in *A Bill for the More General Diffusion of Knowledge*. At one point, Allen writes about two American brothers held in New York by the British. After one brother dies, the other approaches Allen and asks him whether he should "deceive the British by enlisting, and [then] deserting the first opportunity." Allen, not afraid of disguises and "strategem[s]" himself, tells the young man he should. Allen then reflects on the incident:

> [I]t seems that [the two brothers] could not be stimulated to such exertions of heroism from ambition, as they were but obscure soldiers; strong indeed must the internal principle of virtue be, which supported them to brave death, and one of them went through the operation, as did many hundred others.

He refers to this sort of behavior as "public virtue" and portrays himself as one of its greatest exemplars, along with Washington, John Fell, and numerous others whose brief stories Allen embeds in his own. In this sense, Allen intends his written life to counteract selfishness and ambition, teaching instead the "virtue" and honor of liberty, sociability, openness, and equality. Though it may seem like self-aggrandizement to us, Allen's behavior should be read in context as the selfless expression of American liberty.

Allen's notion that virtue is disinterested creates tension in the narrative, a tension that can allow Williams to read his actions as "self-creation" and, at the same time, me to read his actions as "self-less." When, for example, a year into captivity, Allen continues to insist that his "rank" entitles him to preferential treatment, he juxtaposes a British class-based notion with an American republican one. "I now found myself on parole," he writes at one point, ". . . where I soon projected means to live in some measure agreeable to my rank, though I was destitute of cash." What merit or virtue or honor entitles him to more than the two brothers whose "internal principle of virtue" stimulated them to heroism? The proprieties of class should, in Allen's republican vision, be unrelated to true virtue. But they never are; Allen desires "rank" and its accoutrements even as he suggests that they are vestiges of an outmoded hierarchical system. Allen himself never consciously recognizes this tension, though elsewhere he quite clearly states the republican ideal: "I shared the same fate with the [other prisoners], and though they offered me more than an even share, I refused to accept it, as it was a time of substantial distress, which in my opinion I ought to partake equally with the rest, and set an example of virtue and fortitude to our little commonwealth." Here, equality of merit, combined with dehumanizing conditions, equalizes men, creating a commonwealth that mirrors the larger commonwealth that their suffering is intended to help bring into being.

Virtue and reputation, seen through a specifically republican lens, are thus central to Allen's notion of gentlemanly behavior. The other trait that defines gentlemanliness for him is sentimentality. Allen's *Narrative* returns again and again to feelings: "This I could not reconcile to my own feelings as a man, much less as an officer"; "The guard which was set over us, was by this time touched with feelings of compassion"; "I . . . am sure that I express the sentiments and feelings of all the friends to the present revolution." When Captain Smith first offers to treat Allen as a gentleman, Allen responds as would many fictional characters from British novels of the 1760s and 1770s: "This was so unexpected and sudden a transition, that it drew tears from my eyes, (which all the ill usage I had before met with, was not able to produce) nor could I at first hardly speak." This is one of the genuine signs offered by Allen in the course of the narrative—genuine because spontaneous, physical, and uncontrollable—and it contrasts to other blustering actions that some readers take for the "real" Allen, such as his cursing, his legendary exploits, and his rustic frontier clothing. (Not only does Allen often tell us that those other actions are disguises, as when he says that it was "political to act in some measure the madman," but they are always characterized by Allen's forethought and control. Allen's "strategem[s]" are poses designed to speak within specific, local, and temporary contexts. I shall have more to say about this in a moment.)

The "sensible feelings of humanity" that Allen and others like him wear on their sleeves were very much in vogue in England and America in the 1770s and 1780s. No matter how one understands the origins of the vogue, Allen's use of sentimental language places him squarely within a group of fictional characters who dominate the Anglo-American literary scene well into the 1780s: Harley (in Henry Mackenzie's *The Man of Feeling*, 1771), Mr. Yorick (in Laurence Sterne's *A Sentimental Journey*, 1768), Sir George Ellison (in Sarah Scott's *The Man of Real Sensibility*, 1766), Werther (in Johann Wolfgang Goethe's *The Sorrows of Young Werther*, 1774), and Dr. Primrose (in Oliver Goldsmith's *The Vicar of Wakefield*, 1766). These novels were both imported from abroad and reprinted in the colonies. Sterne's *A Sentimental Journey*, for example, was reprinted three times in the American colonies prior to 1778, when Allen began to write his *Narrative*. All five works cited above went through three or more American editions alone by the end of the century, in addition to being imported in English editions. It is not yet clear to me, I must admit, where Allen picks up the language of sentimentality and sensibility. Jellison, his most reliable biographer, reports that Allen read no more than "a half-dozen" books in his entire life (14). But the narrator of Allen's *Narrative* is, nevertheless, a sentimentalist, a man of feeling.

That sentimentality is a trait shared by gentlemen is pointed out at numerous times in the narrative. A captain named (ironically) Royal tells Allen that "his express orders were to treat [Allen] with . . . severity, which was disagreeable to his own feelings"; Royal can never bring himself to "insult" Allen, even though "many others who came on board did." Before Captain Smith ever comes to Allen's aid, his commanding officer upbraids him for sympathizing with a "severe" letter in which Allen, demanding "gentleman-like usage," gave "the British . . . their true character." Do "you take the part of a rebel against me?" the commanding officer asks Smith. Smith responds that "he rather spoke his sentiments." Simply put, the "true character" of some of the British officers is that they cannot feel. In one instance, Allen tries to gain the aid of a purser on a ship. After his request for stores is denied, Allen tries "to reason the matter with [the purser]." Unsuccessful, Allen then "held [the purser's] honor up to view . . . but found his honor impenetrable." Unsuccessful, Allen next "endeavored to touch his humanity, but found he had none." Reason, honor, and humanity are different aspects of the self, located at deeper and deeper levels of being. Other officers, however, and Allen himself reach out to others with honor and humanity, figured by Allen as generosity, charity, benevolence, sentiment, and sympathetic friendship. One captain (Allen cannot remember his name) tells Allen that "there is a greatness of soul for personal friendship to subsist between you and me." These two men have opened their innermost recesses to each other, and come disease, imprisonment, poverty, and destitution, that connection persists. Allen remakes the world in his *Narrative* so that the ideal community is grounded in sensibility not reason, in feeling not intellect.

Allen's *Narrative* is like no other document from the war years so much as it is like Thomas Jefferson's draft of the Declaration of Independence. The historian Garry Wills has studied Jefferson's Declaration as a "sentimental paper" (257–319), focusing quite rightly on Jefferson's use of such language as "agonizing affection," "unfeeling brethren," and "bands which have connected" people. Wills locates the origins of

Jefferson's thinking in Scottish Common Sense philosophy and, perhaps more surprisingly, given Jefferson's mistrust of the novel, in Laurence Sterne. In the Declaration, Wills shows us, Jefferson presents evidence of insensitive, unnatural behavior on the part of the English, particularly of the king's desire to create an "absolute tyranny" over the American states, heretofore his dutiful children. "To prove this let facts be submitted to a candid world," Jefferson writes. Allen grounds his *Narrative* in the same rhetorical move. "I took [care]," he says at one point, "to inform myself . . . of the very design and aims of Gen. Howe and his council: the latter of which I predicated on the former, and submit it to the candid public." Allen's descriptions of physical punishment, of deprivation, "of the assuming tyranny, and the haughty, malevolent, and insolent behavior of the enemy [from 1776 to 1778]" rise in crescendo in the course of the narrative. Like Jefferson, he wants to appeal to his audience by virtue of the sheer number of instances of depraved behavior, and also through the rhetoric of wounded sensibility that gives those facts their true meaning. Jefferson, accordingly, has the king of England "plundering" seas and "ravaging" coasts, waging "cruel war against human nature itself" and "prostituting" his negative (that is, abusing his veto on colonial legislation); he makes the people of Great Britain "deaf to the voice of justice & of consanguinity" and, like unfeeling brothers, willing to ignore a sibling's "agonizing affection"; and he imagines the American audience as moved, as injured, as wounded by the ungenerous, unnatural, unfeeling behavior of the king and people. Allen's focus is on the unnatural and unfeeling British commanders and soldiers; by 1779, of course, the king had been effectively "killed"—that is, removed from the people's mind as a symbol of the father who controls his family—and what was needed was a vilification of the enemy to encourage enlistments and continued sacrifice. Allen provides just such a vilification. His ideal audience in 1779 is a sympathetic, sensitive American people who, once informed of the truth of the facts, for which Allen, like Jefferson and other eighteenth-century gentlemen, "stake[s] my honor," will respond with emotions and, then, with action.

In a letter written late in his life to Henry Lee, Jefferson claimed that the "object" of the Declaration of Independence was

> Not to find out new principles, or new arguments, never before thought of, not merely to say things which had never been said

> before; but to place before mankind the common sense of the subject, in terms so plain and firm as to command their assent, and to justify ourselves in the independent stand we [were] compelled to take. Neither aiming at originality of principle or sentiment, nor yet copied from any particular or previous writing, it was intended to be an expression of the American mind.

Jefferson's object as he remembered it was quite similar to Allen's in 1779. Allen was not writing an original self into narrative being, nor did he see himself within a tradition of previous self-biographical selves. He attempts to frame the revolution as a conflict between head and heart, between inhuman/inhumane men and—*novus ordo seclorum*, the "new order of the ages"—the feeling, generous, sentimental revolutionaries. "If our country," Jefferson wrote in a famous letter to his close friend Maria Cosway in 1786, "when pressed with wrongs at the point of the bayonet, had been governed by [its] heads instead of [its] hearts, where should we have been now? Hanging on a gallows as high as Haman's." Hanging and dismemberment were the punishment for treason in Great Britain in the eighteenth century. Allen knew that: his first inhumane British persecutor tells him he "shall grace a halter at Tyburn." That he did not hang is, indeed, attributable in his own account of his captivity to his heart.

The self-biographical Ethan Allen is, then, virtuous, gentlemanly, and sentimental. Like Royall Tyler's stage creation a few years later, Col. Manly in *The Contrast* (1787), Allen is "manly" in the eighteenth-century's sense of that word. Within the plot of the narrative, during the thirty-four months of his captivity, Allen asserts that this identity is constant: removed from jail to a general's quarters near the time of his release, he remarks "that I was the same man still." Captive or free, jailed or paroled, he is "the same man still." The process by which he became this fixed identity is not presented in the narrative; Allen, in a sense, leaps fully formed onto the first page of the *Narrative*. We can, however, infer the development of this self from two key moments in the narrative, one at the beginning and one at the end. The moments frame Allen's *Narrative* and are, quite clearly, ways for him to "enter" and "exit" the story.

"Ever since I arrived to a state of manhood," Allen begins, "and acquainted myself with the general history of mankind, I have felt a sincere passion for liberty." Reading the "history of nations doomed to perpetual slavery" because their people yielded "their natural

born liberties" to "tyrants," Allen reacts with what he terms a "philosophical horror." We have no way of knowing what histories Allen
has in mind here: he himself, remember, admittedly "missed a liberal
education," his biographers report that he read very little, and the
Narrative itself yields very few (if any) classical or contemporaneous
literary references. The Bible is really the only written text that Allen
alludes to in the *Narrative*. The historian Bernard Bailyn reminds us
that, though the writers of the revolutionary generation drew citations
from a whole range of classical authors, most colonists had "detailed
knowledge and engaged interest" in "only one era and one small
group of writers. . . . [that is,] the political history of Rome" from the
early first century B.C. to the end of the second century A.D. (*Ideological Origins* 25). It was from that period, which includes Brutus's assassi-
nation of the tyrant Caesar, formerly his friend, that the revolutionary
generation derived a sense of their purpose in the battle with Britain.
As for eighteenth-century historical influences, Trenchard and Gordon's
Cato's Letters (1721) were well known, as were works by Molesworth,
Molyneux, Macauley, Bolingbroke, and others. Gibbon's magisterial *The
Rise and Fall of the Roman Empire*, coincidentally, began to be published
in 1776. However, Allen does not offer us anything more precise
about his own reading than his comment on nations "doomed to perpetual slavery" by giving up their liberties to tyrants. Still, we can, I
think, safely read his reference as a republican one. He, like many
other Americans, read the conflict as one in which patriotic republicans
resisted the tyranny of a dictator (George III or Caesar) who wished
to "enslave" them. Republicans, in this context—or Whigs, as they were
sometimes called—were citizens who believed that the state should be
run by virtuous men selected freely by gentlemen of property. These
republicans set themselves defiantly against systems of government that
allowed "tyrannous" individuals (like kings) or groups (like Parliament) to exercise unreasonable, unequal powers. Republicans feared
tyrants on the one hand, universal democracy on the other.

Note what Allen says next. The clash at Lexington in 1775 was "the
first systematical and bloody attempt . . . to enslave America." He echoes
the paranoia of Jefferson in the Declaration of Independence, as when
Jefferson says that "the history of the present king of Great Britain is
a history of unremitting injuries & usurpations" all of which have as
a "direct object the establishment of an absolute tyranny over these

states." Another historian, Gordon Wood, has quite rightly noted that such paranoia is endemic in the writings of the revolutionaries. Allen says that that event, in light of his reading in what is apparently the Whig, republican tradition, "thoroughly electrified my mind, and fully determined me to take part with my country." This figure of electrification is not repeated or alluded to elsewhere in the *Narrative*, so it is difficult to know how much to make of it. On one level, of course, Allen means that he was shocked or startled or thrilled by his perception that events in 1775 could be made comprehensible by his previous reading. At the same time, however, the figure invokes the inventor Benjamin Franklin, another revolutionary, who discovered in his experiments in the 1740s and 1750s that lightning and electricity were the same element. In 1778, the French sculptor Turgot wrote famously of Franklin, then in France on a diplomatic mission, *Eripuit coelo fulmen sceptrumque tyrannis* ("He snatched the lightning from the sky and the sceptre from tyrants"). In his study of the French Revolution, Simon Schama has noted how "the link between the fall of tyrants and celestial fire" in Turgot's inscription suggested "that liberty was a natural and hence ultimately irresistible force, and contributed further to a growing polarity between things natural . . . and things artificial" (46) in the late eighteenth century. Schama writes about pre-revolutionary France, but his insight is relevant here. Allen's "electrification" at the very beginning of his narrative overtly links three distinct elements: manhood, reading (in a Whig, republican tradition), and the American Revolution. Manhood, in this context, is natural, something to which Allen "arrived"; it is a natural state that requires only time to achieve. As the German philosopher Immanuel Kant put it in a short essay, "What Is Enlightenment," written in 1784, "Enlightenment is man's release from his self-incurred tutelage." Reading history from a Whig, republican perspective is presented as something of a natural process: Allen "acquainted [him]self with the general history of mankind" and unproblematically reads therein the pattern of nations yielding liberty to tyrants. To "take part with my country," then—or, seen from the other side, to rebel against the king of England—follows naturally from these conditions; the conditions, we might say, naturally "electrise" Allen:

> To electrise plus or minus, no more needs to be known than this, that the parts of the tube or sphere that are rubbed, do, in the instant

> of the friction, attract the electrical fire, and therefore take it from
> the thing rubbing: the same parts immediately, as the friction upon
> them ceases, are disposed to give up the first they have received, to
> any body that has less.

So Benjamin Franklin wrote at mid-century, describing one of his world-famous experiments in electricity. Liberty, to switch metaphors, is contagious among Whig men, crossing—like sympathy or electricity itself—from person to person without regard to rank, national origin, or religion. Franklin, Kant once remarked, was a new Prometheus who had stolen fire from the heavens. It was a fire that could reach through books and events to convert or transform farmboys into exemplars of liberty.

Near the end of his narrative, Allen is converted again. In what might seem at first a curious decision, he inserts General John Burgoyne's 1777 *Proclamation* to the inhabitants of America "as a specimen of [England's] arrogance." Burgoyne claims that the rebels are arbitrary, tyrannical, and unnatural, and he calls upon Americans to welcome and aid his troops in their tireless efforts to "re-establish . . . the blessings of a legal government." In the narrative itself, his *Proclamation* comes on the heels of Allen's extended description of the many "murders and cruelties" committed by the king's commanders and troops in America and so is meant to reveal, ironically, the hypocrisy of England. Not only is England "opulent, puissant and haughty," but in its "vanity" it has no qualms about hypocritically adopting the language of sentimental republicanism to achieve its enslavement of America. In using such language to describe the Tories, Burgoyne's *Proclamation* exposes the hypocrisy of phrases like "affecting interest" and "friends to liberty," both because Allen's extended description of Tory behavior belies their meaning and because Burgoyne himself ends the *Proclamation* by attempting to frighten Americans with his suggestion that he has "but to give stretch to the Indian forces under [his] direction" to overtake America. The "affecting interest" of friends, any sentimentalist could have told Burgoyne, cannot be moved by threats or intimidation.

The *Proclamation* initiates a three-page meditation by Allen, which he ends by declaring his true "feelings" for England: "as a nation I hate and despise you," he writes, despite the presence in the nation of some Englishmen "who still retain their virtue." "Virtue, wisdom and policy," Allen points out, always, "in the nature of things," direct national power, and when they are departed, as in England's case, then that nation's "glory is departed." Severing the ties to England, as Jefferson and Paine had done in 1776, Allen then commits himself to a new affectional relationship: "My affections are frenchified." The verb indicates, as did "electrified" earlier, a conversion from one state of being to another. Then, it was the mind that was altered; it was a way of looking at the world and at the affairs of men that changed. Now, it is the emotions, the affections, the heart. The feelings have changed.

Allen intends that this conversion be an analogue to the United States' foreign policy in 1778—that is, that he be understood as saying that his affections will be directed toward any state "courteous" enough to accept his feelings and sentiments. He is not saying that he has become French, or that he wishes to become French (although, indeed, he claims to be studying the French language). "Mankind are naturally too national," he asserts, and it is a function of commerce— on 6 February 1778 American commissioners in Paris signed two treaties with France, one political and one commercial—to permit countries "reciprocally [to] exchange . . . customs and manners," as well as "commodities." Commerce, he says, echoing an English argument that goes back almost one hundred years, erases "the superstition of the mind" formed by local, regional, and national interests, and ties humankind more closely together. Affections, like electricity and like trade, reach across space.

It is at this moment, precisely, that Allen remarks "that I was the same man still." He is "still," in other words, a republican and a sentimentalist. These aspects of the self are essential to the persona depicted in the *Narrative*. They are the center or the core that Allen protects, when threatened, by adopting "stratagem[s]" or ruses. So, for example, in captivity Allen occasionally acts as though he is "delirious"; "my extreme circumstances at certain times, rendered it political to act in some measure the madman." By doing so, he receives better treatment from his captors, allowing his "blood" and "nerves" and "strength" to restore themselves. Because of his behavior, the British "gave out that [he] was crazy, and wholly unmanned," but Allen insists that his "vitals held sound." Within his sentimental system, of course, it is they who have been "unmanned" by ambition, greed, and power.

His stratagems include lying, cursing extravagantly, acting insane, and dressing in rustic clothing. This is behavior that is linked, through the word "stratagem," to General Washington, whose "sagacity" at Princeton in early 1777 "suggested a stratagem to effect that which by force to him was at that time impracticable," namely leaving his campfires burning and marching his men to the British rear where they attacked successfully. Like Washington's, Allen's stratagems are usually performed selflessly: when he feels extreme anxiety about his fate, for example, he conceals it from his fellow prisoners and from the enemy, hoping to "exhibit a good sample of American fortitude" in his "daring soldier-like manner." In another instance, he writes an affecting letter to Congress that he pretends to think will actually be sent; in the letter he describes his ill treatment in captivity but urges Congress to retaliate "not according to the smallness of my character in America, but in proportion to the importance of the cause for which I suffered." The letter, a British officer exultingly tells him, was sent to Lord North instead of Congress. "I had come yankee over him," Allen smugly remarks, for the letter was *supposed* to go to North, where it might "intimidate the haughty English government" by showing the resolve of men like Allen, and where it might, as well, save Allen from hanging.

Allen extends the conception of his narrator as selfless through a series of biblical allusions, the only text that is specifically alluded to in the course of the *Narrative*. The allusions are rarely as dramatic as his demand at Fort Ticonderoga that the British commander surrender "'In the name of the great Jehovah, and the Continental Congress'," but they serve the same purpose of elevating the action of the story to a grand, providential level. Hence Allen's attack on Montreal is "a day of trouble," he and his men endure despicable conditions "about forty days" before their arrival at Falmouth, and Gen. Howe's offer of a large tract of land on the New Hampshire grants resembles Satan's "offer of land to . . . Jesus Christ." These allusions increase in frequency late in the narrative, culminating in Allen's resurrection from the dead at the very end of the *Narrative:* arriving in Bennington on 31 May 1778, "I was to [the Green Mountain Boys] as one rose from the dead."

Ethan Allen's metaphoric resurrection is (locally) into the arms of his feeling comrades—"now both their joy and mine was complete," he writes—and (nationally) into the "rural felicity" of "the rising states of America." Allen rises, and so do the united states. Like Lazarus in the Gospel of John, Allen rises both as a type and as an exhibit. As a type, he stands in for the not-yet-completed revolution in 1779: he shadows forth the triumphant union/reunion that will belong to Americans and, in a way, to all sentimental republicans throughout the world when the revolution finally succeeds. As an exhibit—Lazarus is visual proof of Christ's mediating power for the doubting disciples and friends (John 11.7–44)—Allen stands as a character of or figure for the cluster of ideas his narrative tries to imprint, across space, on the reader's heart: liberty, sentiment, manliness, perseverance.

Exhibition, after all, is a figure that weaves itself in and out of Allen's *Narrative*. Let me return to an incident I cited earlier. The two ministers who discuss "moral philosophy and christianity" with Allen before Pendennis Castle in 1775 lead Allen to note that "such a rebel" as himself "was never before seen in England." He is indeed a "sight." I hoped, he says in another instance, to "exhibit [in my behavior in captivity] a good sample of American fortitude." Allen puts himself and others on display in *The Narrative of Col. Ethan Allen*. From the "monsters" who seem "to wear a phiz of humanity," but are in reality "devils," to the many officers and noncoms who display a true "magnanimity of soul" in their physiognomy, Allen paints visual pictures meant to touch his readers' hearts. A letter he writes on behalf of John Fell, a member of Congress imprisoned by the British, describes his intentions in the *Narrative* itself:

> I therefore wrote a letter to Gen. Robertson, (who commanded in [New York]) and being touched with the most sensible feelings of humanity, which dictated my pen to paint dying distress in such lively colours that it wrought conviction even on the obduracy of a British General, and produced his order to remove the now honourable John Fell, Esqr. out of gaol. . . .

Dictated by "sensible feelings," the pictures Allen paints in his *Narrative* are meant to be affecting, reaching through prejudice and indifference and lassitude to reshape conviction in the hearts of a people that, by 1779, had lost much of its enthusiasm for a lengthy and costly war.

A Note on the Text

The Copley Edition of Ethan Allen's *A Narrative of Colonel Ethan Allen's Captivity* uses the First Edition of 1779, published by Robert Bell of Philadelphia. The long "s" has been eliminated throughout, and running quotation marks have been omitted. The double-columned printing of the first edition has not been maintained. A few obvious printing errors have been silently corrected. Otherwise, the text has not been modernized and retains the original spelling, punctuation, capitalization, and italicization of the first edition. (Some of the long italicized sections may have been the result of the shortage of type in war-time Philadelphia.) Allen, as he himself notes, "missed of a liberal education"—by which he means, among other things, that he did not have a college education—and it was thought best to let his words stand as he had them printed.

A Note on "Links"

The Copley Edition of Ethan Allen's *A Narrative of Colonel Ethan Allen's Captivity* includes a number of "Links" to other works and to ideas that demand more elaboration than a simple footnote might allow. These black-bordered pages are insertions by the editor into the text, designed to help the student see ways in which Allen's text is connected to the world around him. They are not the only "links" that could be made, nor are they complete or finished in themselves. Like computer links, they are potentially infinite. They are intended to be both explanatory and suggestive. Allen's *Narrative* was printed without such insertions, of course, and I hope that the "Links" do not detract from the experience of reading the text as a continuous, uninterrupted narrative.

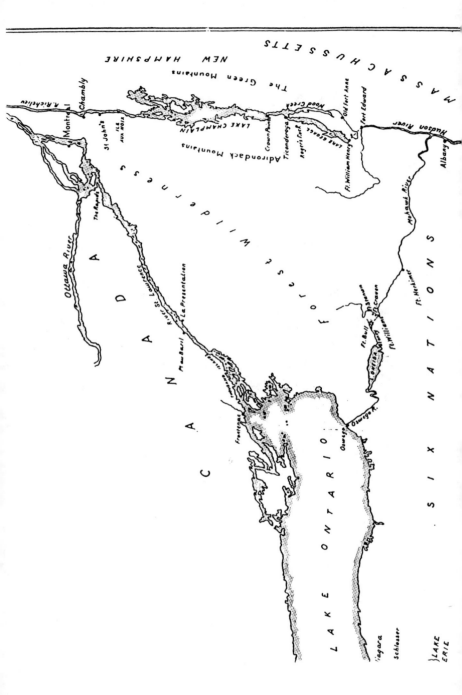

From A.G. Bradley, *The Fight with France for North America.*
London, 1905

A Narrative of Colonel
Ethan Allen's Captivity

Introduction

Induced by a sense of duty to my country, and by the application of many of my worthy friends, some of whom are of the first characters, I have concluded to publish the following narrative of the extraordinary scenes of my captivity, and the discoveries which I made in the course of the same, of the cruel and relentless disposition and behaviour of the enemy, towards the prisoners in their power; from which the state politician, and every gradation of character among the people, to the worthy tiller of the soil, may deduce such inferences as they shall think proper to carry into practice. Some men are appointed into office, in these states, who read the history of the cruelties of this war with the same careless indifferency, as they do the pages of the Roman history; nay, some are preferred to places of trust and profit by the tory influence. The instances are (I hope) but rare; and it stands all freemen in hand, to prevent their further influence, which, of all other things, would be the most baneful to the liberties and happiness of this country; and so far as such influence takes place, robs us of the victory we have obtained, at the expence of so much blood and treasure.

I should have exhibited to the public a history of the facts herein contained, soon after my exchange, had not the urgency of my private affairs, together with more urgent public business, demanded my attention, 'till a few weeks before the date hereof. The reader will readily discern, that a narrative of this sort could not have been wrote when I was a prisoner: My trunk and writings were often searched, under various pretences; so that I never wrote a syllable, or made even a rough minute, whereon I might predicate this narration, but trusted solely to my memory for the whole. I have, however, taken the greatest care and pains to recollect the facts, and arrange them; but as they touch a variety of characters and opposite interests, I am sensible that all will not be pleased with the relation of them: Be this as it will, I have made truth my invariable guide, and stake my honour on the truth of the facts. I have been very generous with the British, in giving them full and ample credit for all their good usage of any considerable consequence, which I met with among them, during my captivity; which was easily done, as I met with but little, in comparison of the bad, which, by reason of the great plurality of it, could not be contained in so concise a narrative; so that I am certain, that I have more fully enumerated the favours which I received, than the abuses I suffered. The critic will be pleased to excuse any inaccuracies in the performance itself, as the author has unfortunately missed of a liberal education.

Bennington, March 25th, 1779

ETHAN ALLEN

A Narrative of
Colonel Ethan Allen's Captivity

Ever since I arrived to a state of manhood, and acquainted myself with the general history of mankind, I have felt a sincere passion for liberty. The history of nations doomed to perpetual slavery, in consequence of yielding up to tyrants their natural born liberties, I read with a sort of philosophical horror; so that the first systematical and bloody attempt at Lexington, to enslave America, thoroughly electrified my mind, and fully determined me to take part with my country: And while I was wishing for an opportunity to signalize myself in its behalf, directions were privately sent to me from the then colony (now state) of Connecticut, to raise the Green Mountain Boys;[1] (and if possible) with them to surprize and take the fortress Ticonderoga.[2] This enterprize I chearfully undertook; and, after first guarding all the several passes that led thither, to cut off all intelligence between the garrison and the country, made a forced march from Bennington, and arrived at the lake opposite to Ticonderoga, on the evening of the ninth day of May, 1775, with two hundred and thirty valiant Green Mountain Boys; and it was with the utmost difficulty that

---

[1] The Green Mountain Boys were armed, organized settlers in the New Hampshire Grants, an area (in present-day southern Vermont) that was claimed in the 1760s and 1770s by both New Hampshire and New York colonies. Having received grants of land from New Hampshire, these settlers resisted New York's efforts to "re-grant" the land to them. Resistance to New York's policy was especially strong west of the Green Mountains, where Allen and others led efforts to expel surveyors, settlers, and judicial officers representing New York.

[2] Fort Ticonderoga was one of several forts strategically located on the Hudson River–Lake George–Lake Champlain waterway leading from Albany, New York, to Montreal, Canada (see previous map).

I procured boats to cross the lake: However, I landed eighty three men near the garrison, and sent the boats back for the rear guard commanded by col. Seth Warner;[3] but the day began to dawn, and I found myself under a necessity to attack the fort, before the rear could cross the lake; and, as it was viewed hazardous, I harangued the officers and soldiers in the manner following: "Friends and fellow-soldiers, you have, for a number of years past, been a scourge and terror to arbitrary power. Your valour has been famed abroad, and acknowledged, as appears by the advice and orders to me (from the general assembly of Connecticut) to surprize and take the garrison now before us. I now propose to advance before you, and in person conduct you through the wicket-gate; for we must this morning either quit our pretensions to valour, or possess ourselves of this fortress in a few minutes; and, in as much as it is a desperate attempt, (which none but the bravest of men dare undertake) I do not urge it on any contrary to his will. You that will undertake voluntarily, poise your firelocks."

The men being (at this time) drawn up in three ranks, each poised his firelock. I ordered them to face to the right; and, at the head of the center-file, marched them immediately to the wicket-gate aforesaid, where I found a centry posted, who instantly snapped his fusee[4] at me: I run immediately toward him, and he retreated through the covered way into the parade within the garrison, gave a halloo, and ran under a bomb-proof. My party who followed me into the fort, I formed on the parade, in such manner as to face the two barracks which faced each other. The garrison being asleep, (except the centries) we gave three huzzas[5] which greatly surprized them. One of the centries made a pass at one of my officers with a charged bayonet, and slightly wounded him: My first thought was to kill him with my sword; but, in an instant, altered the design and fury of the blow to a slight cut on the side of the head; upon which he dropped his gun, and asked quarter,

---

[3] Seth Warner (1743–1784) was, along with Allen, a leader of the Green Mountain Boys. He served actively in the American Revolution from 1775 to 1778, rising to the rank of brigadier-general, but failing health thereafter limited his service.

[4] A light musket or firelock [OED].

[5] A shout of encouragement or triumph; a cheer.

which I readily granted him, and demanded of him the place where the commanding officer kept; he shewed me a pair of stairs in the front of a barrack, on the west part of the garrison, which led up to a second story in said barrack, to which I immediately repaired, and ordered the commander (captain Delaplace) to come forth instantly, or I would sacrifice the whole garrison; at which the captain came immediately to the door with his breeches in his hand, when I ordered him to deliver to me the fort instantly, who asked me by what authority I demanded it: I answered him, "In the name of the great Jehovah, and the Continental Congress." (The authority of the Congress being very little known at that time) he began to speak again; but I interrupted him, and with my drawn sword over his head, again demanded an immediate surrender of the garrison; to which he then complied, and ordered his men to be forthwith paraded without arms, as he had given up the garrison: In the mean time some of my officers had given orders, and in consequence thereof, sundry of the barrack doors were beat down, and about one third of the garrison imprisoned, which consisted of the said commander, a lieutenant Feltham, a conductor of artillery, a gunner, two sergeants, and forty four rank and file; about one hundred pieces of cannon, one 13 inch mortar, and a number of swivels. This surprize was carried into execution in the gray of the morning of the 10th day of May, 1775. The sun seemed to rise that morning with a superior lustre; and Ticonderoga and its dependencies smiled on its conquerors, who tossed about the flowing bowl, and wished success to Congress, and the liberty and freedom of America. Happy it was for me, (at that time) that the then future pages of the Book of Fate, which afterwards unfolded a miserable scene of two years and eight months imprisonment, was hid from my view: But to return to my narration; col. Warner, with the rear guard, crossed the lake, and joined me early in the morning, whom I sent off, without loss of time, with about one hundred men, to take possession of Crown Point, which was garrisoned with a sergeant and twelve men; which he took possession of the same day, as also upwards of one hundred pieces of cannon. But one thing now remained to be done, to make ourselves complete masters of Lake Champlain: This was to possess ourselves of a sloop of war, which was then laying at St. John's; to effect which, it was agreed in a council of war, to arm and man out a certain schooner, which lay at South Bay, and that captain (now general)

LINK

"I . . . ordered the commander (captain Delaplace) to come forth instantly, or I would sacrifice the whole garrison; at which the captain came immediately to the door with his breeches in his hand. . . ."

Contemporary accounts agree that Allen actually made his surrender demand to the junior officer at Fort Ticonderoga, Lieutenant Jocelyn Feltham. Allen may have been embarrassed that he mistook Feltham for Captain Delaplace, or he may have felt that his heroic actions and "gentlemanly" status demanded a capitulation from the commanding officer. In any case, his account differs from that of Lieut. Feltham, who had little reason to lie about the event. Writing to his superiors on June 11, 1775, Feltham reported:

I was awaken'd [that morning] by numbers of shrieks, & the words no quarter, no quarter from a number of arm'd rabble. I jump'd up about which time I heard the noise continue in the area of the fort. I ran undress'd to knock at Capt Delaplaces door & to receive his orders or wake him; the door was fast [i.e. locked]. The room I lay in being close to Capt Delaplaces, I stept back, put on my coat & waist coat & returned to his room, there being no possibility of getting to the men as there were numbers of the rioters on the bastions of the wing of the fort on which the door of my room and back door of Capt Delaplaces room led. With great difficulty, I got into his room being pursued from which there was a door down by stairs in to the area of the fort, I ask'd Capt Delaplace who was now just up what I should do, & offer'd to force my way if possible to our men. On opening this door the bottom of the stairs was filld with the rioters & many were forcing their way up, knowing the Commanding Officer lived there, as they had broke open the lower rooms where the officers live in winter, and could not find them there. From the top of the stairs I endeavour'd to make them hear me, but it was impossible. On making a signal not to come up the stairs, they stop'd, & proclaim'd silence among themselves. I then address'd them, but in a stile not agreeable to them I ask'd them a number of questions, expecting to amuse them till our people fired which I must certainly own I thought would have been the case. After asking them the most material questions I could think viz by what authority they entered his majesties fort who were their leaders what their intent &c &c I was inform'd by one Ethan Allen and one Benedict Arnold that they had a joint command. Arnold informing me he came from instructions

> received from the congress at Cambridge which he afterwards shew'd
> me. Mr Allen told me his orders were from the province of Con-
> necticut & that he must have immediate possession of the fort and
> all the effects of George the third (those were his words) Mr Allen
> insisting on this with a drawn sword over my head & numbers of
> his followers firelocks presented at me alledging I was command-
> ing officer & to give up the fort, and if it was not comply'd with, or
> that there was a single gun fired in the fort neither man woman or
> child should be left alive in the fort. Mr Arnold begg'd it in a genteel
> manner but without success. It was owing to him they were pre-
> vented getting into Capt Delaplaces room, after they found I did
> not command. Capt Delaplace being dress'd came out. . . .

Arnold[6] should command her, and that I should command the batteaux.[7]
The necessary preparations being made, we set sail from Ticonderoga, in
quest of the sloop, which was much larger, and carried more guns
and heavier metal than the schooner. General Arnold, with the
schooner sailing faster than the batteaux, arrived at St. John's; and by
surprize, possessed himself of the sloop, before I could arrive with
the batteaux: He also made prisoners of a sergeant and twelve men,
who were garrisoned at that place. It is worthy remark, that as soon
as general Arnold had secured the prisoners on board, and had made
preparation for sailing, the wind, which but a few hours before was
fresh in the south, and well served to carry us to St. John's, now
shifted, and came fresh from the north; and in about one hour's time,
general Arnold sailed with the prize and schooner for Ticonderoga:
When I met him with my party, within a few miles of St. John's, he
saluted me with a discharge of cannon, which I returned with a vol-
ley of small arms: This being repeated three times, I went on board
the sloop with my party, where several loyal Congress healths were
drank. We were now masters of lake Champlain, and the garrisons
depending thereon. This success I viewed of consequence in the scale
of American politics; for if a settlement between the then colonies and

[6] Benedict Arnold (1741–1801), who later became infamous as a traitor to the
revolutionary cause, was an ardent patriot and able field commander early
in the war. He rose to the rank of major-general in 1777, commanded troops
in several key battles in New York in that year, and was appointed by Washington
as commander of Philadelphia after the British withdrawal from that city in 1778.

[7] A light, flat-bottomed boat (plural).

Great Britain, had soon taken place, it would have been easy to have restored these acquisitions; but viewing the then future consequences of a cruel war, (as it has really proved to be) and the command of that lake, garrisons, artillery, &c. must be viewed to be of signal importance to the American cause, and it is marvellous to me, that we ever lost the command of it. Nothing but the taking a Burgoyne, with a whole British army, could (in my opinion) atone for it;[8] and notwithstanding such an extraordinary victory, we must be obliged to regain the command of that lake again, be the cost what it will: By doing this, Canada will easily be brought into union and confederacy with the United States of America. Such an event would put it out of the power of the western tribes of Indians to carry on a war with us, and be a solid and durable bar against any further inhuman barbarities committed on our frontier inhabitants, by cruel and blood-thirsty savages; for it is impossible for them to carry on a war, except they are supported by the trade and commerce of some civilized nation; which to them would be impracticable, did Canada compose a part of the American empire.

Early in the fall of the year, the little army, under the command of the generals Schuyler[9] and Montgomery,[10] were ordered to advance into Canada. I was at Ticonderoga, when this order arrived; and the general, with most of the field officers, requested me to attend them in the expedition; and tho' at that time, I had no commission from Congress, yet they engaged me, that I should be considered as an officer the same as tho' I had a commission; and should, as occasion might require, command certain detachments of the army.—This I considered as an honourable offer, and did not hesitate to comply with it, and advanced with the army to the isle Aux Noix; from whence I was ordered (by the general) to go in company with major Brown, and

[8] A reference to the series of battles between British troops, led by John Burgoyne, and the Americans, led by Horatio Gates, in the fall of 1777. Burgoyne surrendered to Gates at Saratoga Springs, a decisive American victory that led, in part, to France's 1778 treaties with the United States.

[9] Phillip John Schuyler (1733–1804) was appointed major-general by Congress on 19 June 1775 and commanded the invasion of Canada.

[10] Richard Montgomery (1738–1775) was appointed brigadier-general by Congress on 19 June 1775 and was second in command during the invasion of Canada. He died in the New Year's Eve assault on Quebec.

certain interpreters, through the woods into Canada, with letters to the Canadians, and to let them know, that the design of the army was only against the English garrisons, and not the country, their liberties, or religion:[11] And having, through much danger, negotiated this business, I returned to the isle Auix Noix the fore part of September, when general Schuyler returned to Albany; and in consequence the command devolved upon general Montgomery, whom I assisted in laying a line of circumvallation round the fortress St. John's: After which I was ordered by the general, to make a second tour into Canada, upon nearly the same design as before; and withal to observe the disposition, designs and movements of the inhabitants of the country: This reconnoitre I undertook with reluctance, chusing rather to assist at the siege of St. John's, which was then closely invested; but my esteem for the general's person, and opinion of him as a politician and brave officer, induced me to proceed.

I passed through all the parishes on the river Sorrel, to a parish at the mouth of the same, which is called by the same name, preaching politics; and went from thence across the Sorrel to the river St. Lawrence, and up the river through the parishes to Longale, and so far met with good success as an itinerant.[12] In this round, my guard was Canadians, (my interpreter and some few attendants excepted.) On the morning of the 24th day of September, I set out with my guard of about eighty men, from Longale, to go to Lapraier; from whence I determined to go to general Montgomery's camp; but had not advanced two miles before I met with major Brown, (who has since been advanced to the rank of a colonel) who desired me to halt, saying that he had something of importance to communicate to me and my confidents; upon which I halted the party, and went into an house, and took a private room with him and several of my associates, where col. Brown proposed, that "Provided I would return to Longale,

[11] Canada, which had been settled by the French, was predominantly Catholic. When England defeated France in the Seven Years' War (1755–1763) and took control of Canada as part of the peace settlement, Protestant New Englanders thought that Canada should be forced to become Protestant. However, the Quebec Act of 1774 permitted British Canadians to enjoy full legal rights as Catholics.

[12] An "itinerant" minister is a minister without a settled congregation, one who travels from place to place preaching the word of God.

and procure some canoes, so as to cross the river St. Lawrence a little north of Montreal, he would cross it a little to the south of the town, with near two hundred men, as he had boats sufficient; and that we would make ourselves masters of Montreal."—This plan was readily approved by me and those in council; and in consequence of which I returned to Longale, collected a few canoes, and added about thirty English Americans to my party, and crossed the river in the night of the 24th, agreeable to the before proposed plan. My whole party, at this time, consisted of about one hundred and ten men, near eighty of whom were Canadians. We were the most of the night crossing the river, as we had so few canoes that they had to pass and re-pass three times, to carry my party across. Soon after day-break, I set a guard between me and the town, with special orders to let no person whatever pass or re-pass them, and another guard on the other end of the road, with like directions; in the mean time, I reconnoitered the best ground to make a defence, expecting colonel Brown's party was landed on the other side of the town, he having (the day before) agreed to give three huzzas with his men early in the morning, which signal I was to return, that we might each know that both parties were landed; but the sun, by this time, being near two hours high, and the sign failing, I began to conclude myself to be in a premunire,[13] and would have crossed the river back again, but I knew the enemy would have discovered such an attempt; and as there could not more than one third part of my troops cross at one time, the other two thirds would of course fall into their hands. This I could not reconcile to my own feelings as a man, much less as an officer: I therefore concluded to maintain the ground, (if possible) and all to fare alike. In consequence of this resolution, I dispatched two messengers, one to Lapraire, (to col. Brown) and the other to Lasumption, (a French settlement) to Mr. Walker, who was in our interest, requesting their speedy assistance; giving them at the same time, to understand my critical situation: In the mean time, sundry persons came to my guards, pretending to be friends, but were by them taken prisoners, and brought to me.—These I ordered to confinement, 'till their friendship could be

---

[13] "A situation or condition likened (gravely or humorously) to that of one who has incurred a praemunire [or legal summons]; a difficulty, scrape, fix, predicament" [OED].

further confirmed; for I was jealous they were spies, as they proved to be afterwards: One of the principal of them making his escape, exposed the weakness of my party, which was the final cause of my misfortune; for I have been since informed that Mr. Walker, agreeable to my desire, exerted himself, and had raised a considerable number of men for my assistance, which brought him into difficulty afterwards; but upon hearing of my misfortune, disbanded them again.

The town of Montreal was in a great tumult. Gen. Carlton[14] and the royal party made every preparation to go on board their vessels of force, (as I was afterwards informed) but the spy escaping from my guard to the town, occasioned an alteration in their policy, and emboldened Gen. Carlton to send the force, which he had there collected, out against me. I had previously chosen my ground, but when I saw the number of the enemy, as they sallied out of the town, I perceived it would be a day of trouble, if not of rebuke;[15] but I had no chance to flee, as Montreal was situated on an island, and the river St. Lawrence cut off my communication to Gen. Montgomery's camp. I encouraged my soldiery to bravely defend themselves, that we should soon have help, and that we should be able to keep the ground, if no more. This, and much more I affirmed with the greatest seeming assurance, and which in reality I thought to be in some degree probable.

The enemy consisted of not more than forty regular troops, together with a mixed multitude, chiefly Canadians, with a number of English who lived in the town, and some Indians; in all to the number of near five hundred.

The reader will notice that most of my party were Canadians; indeed it was a motley parcel of soldiery which composed both parties. However, the enemy began the attack from wood-piles, ditches, buildings, and such like places, at a considerable distance, and I returned the fire from a situation more than equally advantageous. The attack began between two and three of the clock in the afternoon,

---

[14] Sir Guy Carlton (1724–1808) was governor of Quebec from 1766 to 1778, and commander in chief of the British forces stationed there. Near the end of the war, he became commander in chief of all British forces in America.

[15] Here, and elsewhere, Allen deliberately adopts biblical language. Compare, for example, Jeremiah 51.2, Ezekiel 7.7, and Psalms 20.1.

just before which I ordered a volunteer, by the name of Richard Young, with a detachment of nine men as a flank guard, which, under the cover of the bank of the river, could not only annoy the enemy, but at the same time, serve as a flank guard to the left of the main body.

The fire continued for some time on both sides; and I was confident that such a remote method of attack, could not carry the ground, (provided it should be continued 'till night:) But near half the body of the enemy began to flank round to my right; upon which I ordered a volunteer, by the name of John Dugan, who had lived many years in Canada, and understood the French language, to detach about fifty of the Canadians, and post himself at an advantageous ditch, which was on my right, to prevent my being surrounded: He advanced with the detachment, but instead of occupying the post, made his escape, as did likewise Mr. Young upon the left, with their detachments. I soon perceived that the enemy was in possession of the ground, which Dugan should have occupied. At this time I had but about forty five men with me; some of whom were wounded: The enemy kept closing round me, nor was it in my power to prevent it; by which means, my situation which was advantageous in the first part of the attack, ceased to be so in the last; and being almost entirely surrounded with such vast unequal numbers, I ordered a retreat, but found that those of the enemy, who were of the country, and their Indians, could run as fast as my men, tho' the regulars could not: Thus I retreated near a mile, and some of the enemy, with the savages, kept flanking me, and others crowded hard in the rear: In fine I expected in a very short time, to try the world of spirits; for I was apprehensive that no quarter would be given to me, and therefore had determined to sell my life as dear as I could: One of the enemy's officers boldly pressing in the rear, discharged his fusee at me; the ball whistled near me, as did many others that day. I returned the salute, and missed him, as running had put us both out of breath; for I conclude we were not frighted: I then saluted him with my tongue in a harsh manner, and told him that inasmuch as his numbers were so far superior to mine, I would surrender, provided I could be treated with honour, and be assured of good quarter for myself and the men who were with me; and he answered I should; another officer coming up directly after, confirmed the treaty; upon which I agreed to surrender with my party, which then consisted of thirty one effective men, and seven wounded. I ordered them to ground their arms, which they did.

The officer I capitulated with, then directed me and my party to advance towards him, which was done; I handed him my sword, and in half a minute after a savage, part of whose head was shaved, being almost naked and painted, with feathers intermixed with the hair of the other side of his head, came running to me with an incredible swiftness; he seemed to advance with more than mortal speed; (as he approached near me, his hellish visage was beyond all description; snakes eyes appear innocent in comparison of his; his features extorted; malice, death, murder, and the wrath of devils and damned spirits are the emblems of his countenance) and in less than twelve feet of me, presented his firelock; at the instant of his present, I twitched the officer to whom I gave my sword, between me and the savage; but he flew round with great fury, trying to single me out to shoot me without killing the officer; but by this time I was near as nimble as he, keeping the officer in such a position that his danger was my defence; but in less than half a minute, I was attacked by just such another imp of hell: Then I made the officer fly around with incredible velocity, for a few seconds of time, when I perceived a Canadian (who had lost one eye, as appeared afterwards) taking my part against the savages; and in an instant an Irishman came to my assistance with a fixed bayonet, and drove away the fiends, swearing by jasus he would kill them. This tragic scene composed my mind. The escaping from so awful a death, made even imprisonment happy; the more so as my conquerors on the field treated me with great civility and politeness.

The regular officers said that they were very happy to see col. Allen: I answered them, that I should rather chose to have seen them at gen. Montgomery's camp. The gentlemen replied, that they gave full credit to what I said, and as I walked to the town, which was (as I should guess) more than two miles, a British officer walked at my right hand, and one of the French noblesse at my left; the latter of which in the action, had his eyebrow carried away by a glancing shot, but was nevertheless very merry and facetious, and no abuse was offered me 'till I came to the barrack-yard at Montreal, where I met general Prescott, who asked me my name, which I told him: He then asked me, whether I was that col. Allen, who took Ticonderoga. I told him I was the very man: Then he shook his cane over my head, calling many hard names, among which he frequently used the word rebel, and put himself in a great rage. I told him he would do well not to cane me, for I was not accustomed to it, and shook my fist at him, telling him that that was the beetle of mortality[16] *for him, if he presumed to strike; upon which capt. M'Cloud of the British, pulled him by the shirt, and whispered to him (as he afterwards told me) to this import; that it was inconsistent with his honour to strike a prisoner. He then ordered a sergeant's command with fixed bayonets to come forward, and kill thirteen Canadians, which were included in the treaty aforesaid.*

It cut me to the heart to see the Canadians in so hard a case, in consequence of their having been true to me; they were wringing their hands, saying their prayers, (as I concluded) and expected immediate death. I therefore stepped between the executioners and the Canadians, opened my cloaths, and told gen. Prescott to thrust his bayonets into my breast, for I was the sole cause of the Canadians taking up arms.

The guard in the mean time, rolling their eye-balls from the general to me, as though impatiently waiting his dread commands to sheath their bayonets in my heart; I could however plainly discern, that he was in a suspence and quandary about the matter: This gave me additional hopes of succeeding; for my design was not to die, but to save the Canadians by a finesse. The general stood a minute, when he made the following reply: "I will not execute you now; but you shall grace a halter at Tyburn,[17] God damn ye."

I remember I disdained his mentioning such a place: I was notwith-standing a little inwardly pleased with the expression, as it significantly conveyed to me the idea of postponing the present appearance of death; beside his sentence was by no means final, as to "gracing a halter," *although I had anxiety about it after I landed in England, as the reader will find in the course of this history. Gen. Prescott then ordered one of his officers to take me on board the Gaspee schooner of War, and confine me, hands and feet, in irons, which was done the same afternoon I was taken.*

The action continued an hour and three quarters by the watch, and I know not to this day how many of my men were killed, though I am certain there were but few; if I remember right, seven were wounded; one of them,

---

[16] A beetle is a heavy mallet with a large wooden head. Allen is threatening to turn Prescott's cane against him.

[17] Tyburn was a place of execution for criminals in England. A halter is a noose, and most capital offenders in England in the eighteenth century were hanged.

William Stewart by name, was wounded by a savage with a tomahawk, after he was taken prisoner and disarmed, but was rescued by some of the generous enemy; and so far recovered his wounds, that he afterwards went with the other prisoners to England.

Of the enemy were killed a major Carden, who had been wounded in eleven different battles, & an eminent merchant Patterson of Montreal, and some others, but I never knew their whole loss, as their accounts were different. I am apprehensive that it is rare, that so much ammunition was expended, and so little execution done by it; though such of my party as stood the ground, behaved with great fortitude, much exceeding that of the enemy, but were not the best of marksmen, and I am apprehensive, were all killed or taken; the wounded were put into the hospital at Montreal, and those that were not, were put on board of different vessels in the river, and shackled together by pairs, viz. two men fastened together by one hand cuff, being closely fixed to one wrist of each of them, and treated with the greatest severity, nay as criminals.

I come now to the description of the irons, which were put on me: The hand cuff was of a common size and form, but my leg irons (I should imagine) would weigh thirty pounds; the bar was eight feet long, and very substantial; the shackles which encompassed my ancles, were very tight. I was told by the officer who put them on, that it was the king's plate, and I heard other of their officers say, that it would weigh forty weight. The irons were so close upon my ancles, that I could not lie down in any other manner than on my back. I was put into the lowest and most wretched part of the vessel, where I got the favour of a chest to sit on; the same answered for my bed at night, and having procured some little blocks of the guard (who day and night, with fixed bayonets, watched over me) to lay under each end of the large bar of my leg irons, to preserve my ancles from galling, while I sat on the chest, or lay back on the same, though most of the time, night and day, I set on it; but at length having a desire to lie down on my side, which the closeness of the irons forbid, desired the captain to loosen them for that purpose, but was denied the favour: The captain's name was Royal, who did not seem to be an ill natured man; but often-times said, that his express orders were to treat me with such severity, which was disagreeable to his own feelings; nor did he ever insult me, though many others, who came on board, did. One of the officers, by the name of Bradley, was very generous to me; he would often send me victuals from his own table; nor did a day fail, but that he sent me a good drink of grog.

The reader is now invited back to the time I was put in irons. I requested the privilege to write to gen. Prescott, which was granted. I reminded him of the kind and generous manner of my treatment to the prisoners I took at Ticonderoga; the injustice and ungentleman-like usage, which I had met with from him, and demanded gentleman like usage, but received no answer from him. I soon after wrote to gen. Carlton, which met the same success. In the mean while many of those who were permitted to see me, were very insulting.

I was confined in the manner I have related, on board the Gaspee schooner, about six weeks; during which time I was obliged to throw out plenty of extravagant language which answered certain purposes, (at that time) better than to grace a history.

To give an instance upon being insulted, in a fit of anger I twisted off a nail with my teeth, which I took to be a ten-penny nail; it went through the mortise of the bar of my hand-cuff, and at the same time I swaggered over those who abused me; particularly a doctor Dace, who told me that I was outlawed by New York,[18] and deserved death for several years past; was at last fully ripened for the halter, and in a fair way to obtain it: When I challenged him, he excused himself in consequence, as he said, of my being a criminal; but I flung such a flood of language at him, that it shocked him and the spectators, for my anger was very great. I heard one say, damn him, can he eat iron? After that a small padlock was fixed to the hand-cuff, instead of the nail; and as they were mean-spirited in their treatment to me, so it appeared to me, that they were equally timorous and cowardly.

I was after sent with the prisoners taken with me to an armed vessel in the river, which lay off against Quebec, under the command of capt. M'Cloud of the British, who treated me in a very generous and obliging manner, and according to my rank; in about twenty four hours I bid him farewell with regret; but my good fortune still continued: The name of the captain of the vessel I was put on board, was Little John; who, with his officers, behaved in a polite, generous, and friendly manner. I lived with them in the cabbin, and fared on the best; my irons being taken off, contrary to the order he had received

---

[18] This is a reference to Allen's actions as a leader of the Green Mountain Boys in the early 1770s.

LINK

". . . I twisted off a nail with my teeth, which I took to be a ten penny nail. . . .I heard one say, damn him, can he eat iron?. . ."

By all contemporary accounts, Ethan Allen was a large, strong-willed, charismatic man, and he lived a rough and oftentimes violent life on the western frontier. Stories of his legendary exploits began to be told during his life, often by his admiring younger brothers, sometimes by himself, as here. However, as Michael Bellesiles writes, "In the years after the Revolution, Allen emerged as one of America's first national figures, an authentic frontier folk hero. Through his unique blend of republicanism, pragmatism, and self-promotion, Allen established himself at the center stage of a dozen revolutionary dramas" (245). Two texts that helped to fix the image of Allen in the American mind were Daniel Thompson's *Green Mountain Boys* (1839), a novel that appeared in fifty editions between 1839 and 1860, and Herman Melville's *Israel Potter* (1854). Thompson's Ethan Allen is a simple farmer, devoid of intellectual pretensions; he is an innocent who is good at tricking New Yorkers and the British. (Clearly, he was modeled on James Fenimore Cooper's Natty Bumppo.) One character in *Green Mountain Boys* remarks about Allen, "Lordy! Why, two Alexanders, with half a dozen Turks thrown in to stiffen the upper lip, would be used up in making the priming to Ethan Allen!" Melville's Ethan Allen is a wild westerner, a symbol of the honesty, intelligence, and simplicity of American frontiersmen. Melville writes, "Allen seems to have been a curious combination of a Hercules, a Joe Miller, a Bayard, and a Tom Hyer; had a person like the Belgian giants; mountain music in him like a Swiss; a heart plump as Coeur de Lion's. Though born in New England, he exhibited no trace of her character. He was frank; bluff; companionable as a Pagan; convivial; a Roman; hearty as a harvest. His spirit was essentially Western; and herein is his peculiar Americanism; for the western spirit is, or will yet be (for no other is, or can be) the true American one."

A shorter-lived tradition saw Ethan Allen as an atheistic philosopher, a loud-mouthed and ill-educated pretender to reason. Lemuel

Hopkins, one of the Connecticut Wits, a group of conservative poets writing during and after the American Revolution, wrote about him:

> Behold him move ye staunch divines!
> His tall head bustling through the pines;
> All front he seems like wall of brass,
> And brays tremendous as an ass;
> One hand is clench'd to batter noses,
> While t'other scrawls 'gainst Paul and Moses.

Timothy Dwight, later president of Yale College, wrote in 1788, "In vain thro realms of nonsense [Allen] ran/The great Clodhopping oracle of man./Yet faithful were his toils: What could he more?/In Satan's cause he bustled, bruised, and swore." This tradition lost its force when conservative, evangelical Christianity began to decline in social influence in the early nineteenth century.

from the commanding officer; but capt. Little John swore, that a brave man should not be used as a rascal, on board his ship.

Thus I found myself in possession of happiness once more, and the evils I had lately suffered, gave me an uncommon relish for it.

Capt. Little John used to go to Quebec almost every day; in order to pay his respects to certain gentlemen and ladies; being there on a certain day, he happened to meet with some disagreeable treatment (as he imagined) from a lieutenant of a man of war, and one word brought on another, 'till the lieutenant challenged him to a duel on the plains of Abraham. Capt. Little John was a gentleman, who entertained a high sense of honour, and could do no less than accept the challenge.

At nine o'clock the next morning they were to fight. The captain returned in the evening, and acquainted his lieutenant and me with the affair: His lieutenant was a high-blooded Scotchman as well as himself, who replied to his captain, that he should not want for a second. With this I interrupted him, and gave the captain to understand, that since an opportunity had presented, I would be glad to testify my gratitude to him, by acting the part of a faithful second, on which he gave me his hand, and said that he wanted no better man. Says he, I am a king's officer, and you a prisoner under my care; you must therefore go with me to the place appointed, in disguise, and added further: "You must engage to me, upon the honour of a gentleman, that whether I die or live, or whatever happens, (provided you live) that you will return to my lieutenant on board this ship." All this I solemnly engaged him. The combatants were to discharge each a pocket-pistol, and then to fall on with their iron-hilted muckle-whangers;[19] and one of that sort was allotted for me; but some British officers, who interposed early in the morning, settled the controversy without fighting.

Now having enjoyed eight or nine days happiness, from the polite and generous treatment of capt. Little John and his officers, I was obliged to bid them farewel, parting with them in as friendly a manner, as we had lived together, which, to the best of my memory, was the eleventh of November: When a detachment of gen. Arnold's little army appeared on point Levy, opposite Quebec, (who had performed an extraordinary march through a wilderness country, with design to have surprized the capital of Canada)[20] I was then taken on board a vessel called the Adamant, together with the prisoners taken with me, and put under the power of an English merchant from London, whose name was Brook Watson;[21] a man of malicious and cruel disposition, and who was probably excited in the exercise of his malevolence, by a junto of tories, who sailed with him to England; among whom were col. Guy Johnson, Col. Closs, and their attendants and associates, to the number of about thirty.

All the ship's crew (col. Closs, in his personal behaviour, excepted) behaved towards the prisoners with that spirit of bitterness, which is the

---

[19] A slang term for a large sword.

[20] The attack on Canada in 1775 was two-pronged: Schuyler's and Montgomery's troops advanced north via Lake Champlain (the usual route to Canada), took Montreal (which they did after Allen's earlier, foolhardy attempt failed), and then proceeded on to Quebec; Arnold's troops forged a new northern route through the almost impenetrable Maine woods and then met up with the other expedition. The New Year's Eve assault on Quebec by the combined forces failed.

[21] Sir Brook Watson (1735–1807) served as commissary in the British Army in the Seven Years' War and then settled in London as a merchant. He was conducting business in Canada when the war broke out. He later became lord mayor of London and was knighted in 1803.

peculiar characteristic of tories, when they have the friends of America in their power, measuring their loyalty to the English king by the barbarity, fraud, and deceit which they exercise towards the whigs.

A small place in the vessel, enclosed with white-oak plank, was assigned for the prisoners, and for me among the rest. I should imagine that it was not more than twenty feet one way, and twenty-two the other: Into this place we were all, to the number of thirty four, thrust and hand cuffed, (two prisoners more being added to our number) and were provided with two excrement tubs; in this circumference we were obliged to eat and perform the office of evacuation, during the voyage to England; and were insulted by every black guard sailor and tory on board, in the cruelest manner; but what is the most surprizing is, that not one of us died in the passage. When I was first ordered to go into the filthy enclosure, thro' a small sort of door, I positively refused, and endeavoured to reason the before named Brook Watson out of a conduct so derogatory to every sentiment of honour and humanity, but all to no purpose, my men being forced into the den already; and the rascal who had the charge of the prisoners, commanded me to go immediately in among the rest: He further added that the place was good enough for a rebel; that it was impertinent for a capital offender to talk of honour or humanity; that any thing short of a halter, was too good for me; and that, that would be my portion soon after I landed in England; for which purpose only I was sent thither. About the same time a lieutenant among the tories, insulted me in a grievous manner, saying, that I ought to have been executed for my rebellion against New York, and spit in my face; upon which (tho' I was hand-cuffed) I sprang at him with both hands, and knocked him partly down, but he scrambled along into the cabin, and I after him; there he got under the protection of some men with fixed bayonets, who were ordered to make ready to drive me into the place aforementioned. I challenged him to fight, notwithstanding the impediments that were on my hands, and had the exalted pleasure to see the rascal tremble for fear; his name I have forgot, but Watson ordered his guard to get me into the place with the other prisoners, dead or alive; and I had almost as leave die as do it, standing it out till they environed me round with bayonets; and brutish, prejudiced, abandoned wretches they were, from whom I could expect nothing but death or wounds: However I told them, that they were good honest fellows; that I could not blame them; that I was only in a dispute with a calicoe merchant,[22] who knew not how to behave towards a gentleman of the military establishment. This was spoke rather to appease them for my own preservation, as well as to treat Watson with contempt; but still I found that they were determined to force me into the wretched circumstances, which their prejudiced, and depraved minds had prepared for me: Therefore rather than die, I submitted to their indignities, being drove with bayonets into the filthy dungeon, with the other prisoners, where we were denied fresh water, except a small allowance which was very inadequate to our wants; and in consequence of the stench of the place, each of us was soon followed with a diarrhoea and fever, which occasioned an intolerable thirst. When we asked for water, we were most commonly (instead of obtaining it) insulted and derided; and to add to all the horrors of the place, it was so dark that we could not see each other, and were overspread with body-lice. We had (notwithstanding these severities) full allowance of salt provisions, and a gill of rum per day;[23] the latter of which was of the utmost service to us, and (probably) was the means of saving several of our lives. About forty days we existed in this manner, when the land's end of England was discovered from the mast head; soon after which the prisoners were taken from their gloomy abode, being permitted to see the light of the sun, and breath fresh air, which to us was very refreshing. The day following we landed at Falmouth.

A few days before I was taken prisoner, I shifted my cloaths, by which I happened to be taken in a Canadian dress, viz. a short fawn skin jacket, double-breasted, an under vest and breeches of sagathy, worsted stockings, a decent pair of shoes, two plain shirts, and a red worsted cap: This was all the cloathing I had, in which I made my appearance in England.

When the prisoners were landed, multitudes of the citizens of Falmouth (excited by curiosity) crowded together to see us, which was equally gratifying to us. I saw numbers of people on the tops of houses, and

---

[22] Calico is a cotton cloth. Allen is insulting Watson by suggesting that he is "merely" a merchant (and therefore not a gentleman) and one who, in addition, deals "only" in petty items, like cloth.

[23] A "gill" is one-quarter of a pint, or four fluid ounces.

the rising adjacent grounds were covered with them of both sexes: The throng was so great, that the king's officers were obliged to draw their swords, and force a passage to Pendennis castle which was near a mile from the town, where we were closely confined, in consequence of orders from gen. Carlton, who then commanded in Canada.

The rascally Brook Watson then set out for London in great haste, expecting the reward of his zeal; but the ministry received him (as I have been since informed) rather coolly; for the minority in parliament took advantage, arguing that the opposition of America to Great Britain, was not a rebellion: If it is, (say they) why do you not execute col. Allen, according to law? but the majority argued, that I ought to be executed, and that the opposition was really a rebellion, but that policy obliged them not to do it, inasmuch as the Congress had then most prisoners in their power; so that my being sent to England, for the purpose of being executed, and necessity restraining them, was rather a soil on their laws and authority, and they consequently disapproved of my being sent thither: But I never had heard the least hint of those debates, (in parliament) or of the working of their policy, 'till some time after I left England.[24]

Consequently the reader will readily conceive I was anxious about my preservation, (knowing that I was in the power of a haughty and cruel nation, considered as such.) Therefore the first proposition which I determined in my own mind was, that humanity and moral suasion would not be consulted in the determining of my fate: And those that daily came in great numbers, out of curiosity to see me, both gentle and simple, united in this, that I would be hanged. A gentleman from America, by the name of Temple, (and who was friendly to me) just whispered me in the ear, and told me, that bets were laid in London, that I would be executed; he likewise privately gave me a guinea, but durst say but little to me.

However, agreeable to my first negative proposition, that moral virtue would not influence my destiny, I had recourse to stratagem, which I was in hopes would move in the circle of their policy. I

[24] The punishment for treason in Great Britain at that time called not just for death, usually by hanging, but for dismemberment as well. The debate in Parliament in late 1775 focused on what to call the outbreak of hostilities: if a rebellion, then all supporters of the American cause were treasonous. On 23 August 1775, George III declared the colonies in "open and avowed rebellion."

requested of the commander of the castle the privilege of writing to Congress, who, after consulting with an officer that lived in town, of a superior rank, permitted me to write. I wrote, in the fore part of the letter, a short narrative of my ill treatment; but withal let them know, that tho' I was treated as a criminal in England, and continued in irons, together with those taken with me, yet it was in consequence of the orders which the commander of the castle received from general Carlton; and therefore desired Congress to desist from matters of retaliation, 'till they should know the result of the government at England, respecting their treatment towards me, and the prisoners with me, and govern themselves accordingly, with a particular request, that if retaliation should be found necessary, that it might be exercised not according to the smallness of my character in America, but in proportion to the importance of the cause for which I suffered.— This is, according to my present recollection, the substance of the letter subscribed *To the illustrious Continental Congress.* This letter was wrote with a view that it should be sent to the ministry at London, rather than to Congress, with a design to intimidate the haughty English government, and screen my neck from the halter.

The next day the officer (from whom I obtained licence to write) came to see me, and frowned on me on account of the impudence of the letter, (as he phrased it) and further added, "Do you think that we are fools in England, and would send your letter to Congress, with instructions to retaliate on our own people. I have sent your letter to lord North."[25]—This gave me inward satisfaction, (though I carefully concealed it with a pretended resentment) for I found I had come Yankee over him,[26] and that the letter had gone to the identical person I designed it for. Nor do I know (to this day) but that it had the desired effect, though I have not heard any thing of the letter since.

My personal treatment by lieut. Hamilton, who commanded the castle, was very generous. He sent me every day a fine breakfast and dinner from his own table, and a bottle of good wine. Another aged gentleman, whose name I cannot recollect, sent me a good supper:

[25] Frederick North, Lord North (1732–1792), was Chancellor of the Exchequer and First Lord of the Treasury (in effect, prime minister) at the time.

[26] To "come Yankee" over someone is to outsmart him or her.

But there was no distinction in public support between me and the privates; we all lodged on a sort of Dutch bunks, in one common apartment, and were allowed straw. The privates were well supplied with fresh provision, and (with me) took effectual measures to rid ourselves of lice.

I could not but feel inwardly extreme anxious for my fate.—This I however concealed from the prisoners, as well as from the enemy, who were perpetually shaking the halter at me. I nevertheless treated them with scorn and contempt; and having sent my letter to the ministry, could conceive of nothing more in my power but to keep up my spirits, behave in a daring soldier-like manner, that I might exhibit a good sample of American fortitude. Such a conduct (I judged) would have a more probable tendency to my preservation than concession and timidity. This, therefore, was my deportment, and I had lastly determined, (in my own mind) that if a cruel death must inevitably be my portion, I would face it undaunted, and tho' I greatly rejoice that I have returned to my country and friends, and to see the power and pride of Great Britain humbled; yet I am confident I could (then) die without the least appearance of dismay.

I now clearly recollect that my mind was so resolved, that I would not have trembled or shewn the least fear, as I was sensible it could not alter my fate, nor do more than reproach my memory, make my last act despicable to my enemies, and eclipse the other actions of my life. For I reasoned thus, that nothing was more common than for men to die, with their friends round them, weeping and lamenting over them, but not able to help them, which was in reality not different in the consequence of it from such a death as I was apprehensive of: And as death was the natural consequence of animal life, to which the laws of nature subject mankind, to be timorous and uneasy as to the event or manner of it, was inconsistent with the character of a philosopher or soldier. The cause I was engaged in, I ever viewed worthy hazarding my life for, nor was I (at the most critical moments of trouble) sorry that I engaged in it; and as to the world of spirits, though I knew nothing of the mode or manner of it, expected nevertheless, when I should arrive at such a world, that I should be as well treated as other gentlemen of my merit.

Among the great numbers of people, who came to the castle to see the prisoners, some gentlemen told me, that they had come fifty miles on purpose to see me, and desired to ask me a number of questions, and to make free with me in conversation. I gave for answer, that I chose freedom in every sense of the word: Then one of them asked me, what my occupation in life had been? I answered him, that in my younger days I had studied divinity, but was a conjurer by profession. He replied, that I conjured wrong at the time that I was taken; and I was obliged to own, that I mistook a figure at that time, but that I had conjured them out of Ticonderoga. This was a place of great notoriety in England, so that the joke seemed to go in my favour.

It was a common thing for me to be taken out of close confinement, into a spacious green in the castle, or rather parade, where numbers of gentlemen and ladies were ready to see and hear me. I often entertained such audiences, with harangues on the impracticability of Great Britain's conquering the (then) colonies of America. At one of these times I asked a gentleman for a bowl of punch, and he ordered his servant to bring it, which he did, and offered it me, but I refused to take it from the hand of his servant; he then gave it to me with his own hand, refusing to drink with me in consequence of my being a state criminal: However I took the punch and drank it all down at one draught, and handed the gentleman the bowl: This made the spectators as well as myself merry. I expatiated on American freedom: This gained the resentment of a young beardless gentleman of the company, who gave himself very great airs, and replied, that he "knew the Americans very well, and was certain that they could not bear the smell of powder." I replied, that I accepted it as a challenge, and was ready to convince him on the spot, that an American could bear the smell of powder; at which he answered, that he should not put himself on a par with me. I then demanded of him to treat the character of the Americans with due respect: He answered that I was an Irishman; but I assured him, that I was a *full blooded Yankee*, and in fine, bantered him so much, that he left me in possession of the ground, and the laugh went against him. Two clergymen came to see me, and inasmuch as they behaved with civility, I returned them the same: We discoursed on several parts of moral philosophy and christianity; and they seemed to be surprized, that I should be acquainted with such topics, or that I should understand a syllogism or regular mode of argumentation.[27] I

---

[27] A syllogism is a form of deductive reasoning, one of the "formal" modes of reasoning taught at colleges and universities in the eighteenth century.

am apprehensive my Canadian dress contributed not a little to the surprize, and excitement of curiosity: To see a gentleman in England, regularly dressed and well behaved, would be no sight at all; but such a rebel, as they were like to call me, it is probable was never before seen in England.

The prisoners were landed at Falmouth a few days before Christmas, and ordered on board the Solebay frigate, captain Symonds, the eighth day of January, 1776, when our hand-irons were taken off. This remove was in consequence (as I have been since informed) of a writ of habeas corpus, which had been procured by some gentleman in England, in order to obtain me my liberty.

The Solebay with sundry other men of war, and about forty transports, rendezvoused at the cove of Cork in Ireland, to take in provision and water.

When we were first brought on board, captain Symonds ordered all the prisoners, and most of the hands on board, to go on the deck, and caused to be read in their hearing, a certain code of laws, or rules for the regulation and ordering of their behaviour; and then in a sovereign manner, ordered the prisoners, me in particular, off the deck, and never to come on it again; for said he, this is a place for gentlemen to walk. So I went off, an officer following me, who told me, that he would shew me the placed allotted for me, and took me down to the cable tire,[28] saying to me, this is your place.

Prior to this I had taken cold, by which I was in an ill state of health, and did not say much to the officer; but stayed there that night, consulted my policy, and found I was in an evil case; that a captain of a man of war was more arbitrary than a king, as he could view his territory with a look of his eye, and a movement of his finger commanded obedience. I felt myself more desponding than I had done at any time before; for I concluded it to be a governmental scheme, to do that clandestinely, which policy forbid to be done under sanction of public justice and law.

However, two days after I shaved and cleansed myself as well as I could, and went on deck: The captain spoke to me in a great rage, and said, "Did I not order you not to come on deck?" I answered him,

---

[28] The cable tier is the part of the ship where cables and spare rigging are stored.

that at the same time he said, "That it was the place for gentlemen to walk;" That I was colonel Allen, but had not been properly introduced to him. He replied, "G-d damn you, Sir, be careful not to walk the same side of the deck that I do." This gave me encouragement, and ever after that, I walked in the manner he had directed, except when he (at certain times afterwards) ordered me off in a passion, and then would directly afterwards go on again, telling him to command his slaves, that I was a gentleman, and had a right to walk the deck; and when he expressly ordered me off, I obeyed, not out of obedience to him, but to set an example to his ship's crew, who ought to obey him.

To walk to the windward side of the deck, is according to custom the prerogative of the captain of the man of war, though he oftentimes, nay commonly walks with his lieutenants, when no strangers are by: When a captain from some other man of war, comes on board, the captains walk to the windward side, and the other gentlemen to the leeward.

It was but a few nights I lodged in the cable-tire, before I gained an acquaintance with the master of arms; his name was Gillegan, an Irishman, who was a generous and well-disposed man, and in a friendly manner, made me a proffer of living with him in a little birth, which was allotted him between decks, and enclosed with canvas; his preferment on board was about equal to that of a sergeant in a regiment. I was comparatively happy in the acceptance of his clemency, and lived with him in friendship, 'till the frigate anchored in the harbour of cape Fear, North Carolina, in America.

Nothing of material consequence happened 'till the fleet rendezvoused at the cove of Cork, (except a violent storm which brought old hardy sailors to their prayers.) It was soon rumoured in Cork that I was on board the Solebay, with a number of prisoners from America; upon which Messrs. Clark and Hay, merchants in company, and a number of other benevolently disposed gentlemen, contributed largely to the relief and support of the prisoners, who were thirty-four in number, and in very needy circumstances. A suit of cloaths from head to foot, including an over coat, or surtout, and two shirts, were bestowed on each of them. My suit I received in superfine broadcloth, sufficient for two jackets, and two pair of breeches overplus of a suit throughout, eight fine Holland shirts and stocks ready made, with a number of pairs of silk and worsted hose, two pair of shoes, two beaver hats, one of which was sent me richly laced with gold, by Mr. James Bonwell. The Irish gentlemen furthermore made a large gratuity of wines of the best sort, old spirits, Geneva,[29] loaf and brown sugar, coffee, tea and chocolate; with a large round of pickled beef, and a number of fat turkies, with many other articles (for my sea-stores) too tedious to mention here. To the privates they bestowed to each man two pounds of tea, and six pounds of brown sugar. These articles were received on board, (at a time when the captain and first lieutenant were gone on shore) by permission of the second lieutenant, a handsome young gentleman, who was then under twenty years of age; his name was Douglass, the son of Admiral Douglass (as I was informed).

As this munificence was so unexpected and plentiful, I may add needful, it impressed on my mind the highest sense of gratitude towards my benefactors; for I was not only supplied with the necessaries and conveniences of life, but with the grandeurs and superfluities of it. Mr. Hays, one of the donators before mentioned, came on board, and behaved in the most obliging manner, telling me, that he hoped my troubles were past, for that the gentlemen of Cork determined to make my sea-stores equal to the captain of the Solebay's; he made a proffer of live stock, and wherewith to support them; but I knew this would be denied: And to crown all, did send to me by another person fifty guineas, but I could not reconcile the receiving the whole to my own feelings, as it might have the appearance of avarice; and therefore received but seven guinea only; and am confident not only from the exercise of the present well-timed generosity, but from a large acquaintance with gentlemen of this nation, that as a people they excel in liberality and bravery.

Two days after the receipt of the aforesaid donations, captain Symonds came on board, full of envy towards the prisoners, and swore by all that is good, that the damned American rebels should not be feasted at this rate, by the damned rebels of Ireland; he therefore took away all my liquors before-mentioned, (except some of the wine which was secreted, and a two gallon jug of old spirits which was reserved for me, per favour of lieutenant Douglass.) The taking my liquors was abominable in his sight; he therefore spoke in my

---

[29] Jenever, or young Dutch gin.

behalf, 'till the captain was angry with him: And in consequence, pro-ceeded & took away all the tea and sugar, which had been given to the other prisoners, and confiscated it to the use of the ship's crew. Our cloathing was not taken away, but the privates were forced to do duty on board. Soon after this there came a boat to the side of the ship, and captain Symonds asked a gentleman that was in it, (in my hearing) what his business was? who answered that he was sent to deliver some sea-stores to colonel Allen, which (if I remember right) he said were sent from Dublin; but the captain damned him very heartily, ordered him away from the ship, and would not suffer him to deliver the stores. I was furthermore informed, that the gentlemen in Cork requested of captain Symonds, that I might be allowed to come into the city, and that they would be responsible I should return to the frigate at a given time, which was denied them.

We sailed from England the 8th day of January, and from the cove of Cork the 12th day of February. Just before we sailed, the prisoners with me were divided, and put on board three different ships of war. This gave me some uneasiness, for they were to a man zealous in the cause of liberty, and behaved with a becoming fortitude in the various scenes of their captivity; but those who were distributed on board other ships of war, were much better used than those that tarried with me, as appeared afterwards.

When the fleet consisting of about forty five sail, including five men of war, sailed from the cove with a fresh breeze, the appearance was beautiful, (abstracted from the unjust and bloody designs they had in view.) We had not sailed many days, before a mighty storm arose, which lasted near twenty-four hours without intermission: The wind blew with relentless fury, and no man could remain on deck, except he was lashed fast, for the waves rolled over the deck by turns, with a forcible rapidity, and every soul on board was anxious for the preservation of the ship, (alias) their lives. In this storm the Thunder-bomb man of war sprang a leak, and was afterwards floated to some part of the coast of England, and the crew saved. We were then said to be in the bay of Biscay. After the storm abated, I could plainly discern that the prisoners were better used for some considerable time.

Nothing of consequence happened after this, 'till we had sailed to the island of Madeira, except a certain favour which I received of captain Symonds, in consequence of an application I made to him, for the privilege of his tailor to make me a suit of cloaths of the cloth bestowed on me in Ireland, which he generously granted. I could then walk the deck with a seeming better grace: When we had reached Madeira, and anchored, sundry gentlemen with the captain went on shore, who I conclude gave the rumour that I was in the frigate; upon which I soon after found Irish generosity was again excited; for a gentleman of this nation sent his clerk on board, to know of me if I would accept a sea-store from him (particularly of wine). This matter I made known to the generous lieutenant Douglass, who readily granted me the favour, provided the articles could be brought on board, during the time of his command; adding that it would be a pleasure to him to serve me, notwithstanding the opposition he met with before: So I directed the gentleman's clerk to inform him, that I was greatly in need of so signal a charity, and desired the young gentleman to make the utmost dispatch, which he did; but in the mean time, capt. Symonds and his officers came on board, and immediately made ready for sailing; the wind at the same time being fair, set sail when the young gentleman was in fair sight with the aforesaid store.

The reader will doubtless recollect the seven guineas I received at the cove of Cork: These enabled me to purchase of the purser what I wanted, had not the captain strictly forbid it, though I made sundry applications to him for that purpose; but his answer to me, when I was sick, was, that it was no matter how soon I was dead, and that he was no ways anxious to preserve the lives of rebels, but wished them all dead; and indeed this was the language of most of the ship's crew. I expostulated not only with the captain, but with other gentlemen on board, on the unreasonableness of such usuage; inferring, that inasmuch as the government in England did not proceed against me as a capital offender, they should not; for that they were by no means impowered by any authority, either civil or military, to do so; for the English government had acquitted me by sending me back a prisoner of war to America, and that they should treat me as such. I further drawed an inference of impolicy on them, provided they should, by hard usage, destroy my life; inasmuch as I might, if living, redeem one of their officers; but the captain replied, that he needed no directions of mine how to treat a rebel; that the British would conquer the American rebels, hang the Congress, and such as promoted the rebellion, (me in particular) and retake their own prisoners; so that my life was of no consequence in the scale of their policy. I gave him for answer, that if they stayed 'till they conquered America, before they hanged me, *I should die of old age,* and desired that 'till such an event took place, he would at least allow me to purchase of the purser, for my own money, such articles as I greatly needed; but he would not permit it, and when I reminded him of the generous and civil usage that their prisoners in captivity in America met with, he said that it was not owing to their goodness, but to their timidity; for said he, they expect to be conquered, and therefore dare not misuse our prisoners, and in fact this was the language of the British officers 'till general Burgoyne was taken, (happy event) and not only of the officers, but of the whole British army. I appeal to all my brother-prisoners, that have been with the British in the southern department, for a confirmation of what I have advanced on this subject. The surgeon of the Solebay, whose name is North, was a very humane and obliging man, and took the best care of the prisoners who were sick.

The third day of May we cast anchor in the harbour of cape Fear in North Carolina, as did Sir Peter Parker's ship of fifty guns a little back of the bar, for there was not depth of water for him to come into the harbour: These two men of war and fourteen sail of transports and others, came after, so that most of the fleet rendezvoused at cape Fear, for three weeks. The soldiers on board the transports were sickly, in consequence of so long a passage; add to this, the small pox carried off many of them: They landed on the main, and formed a camp; but the riflemen annoyed them, and caused them to move to an island in the harbour; but such cursing of riflemen I never heard.

A detachment of regulars was sent up Brunswick river; as they landed, were fired on by those marksmen, and they came back next day, damning the rebels for their unmanly way of fighting, and swearing that they would give no quarter, for they took sight at them, and were behind timber, skulking about. One of the detachments said they lost one man; but a negro man who was with them, and heard what was said, soon after told me that he helped to bury thirty-one of them: This did me some good to find my countrymen giving them battle; for I never heard such swaggering as among general Clinton's little army, (who commanded at that time)[30] and I am apt to think there were four thousand men, though not two thirds of them fit for duty. I heard numbers of them say, that the trees in America should hang well with fruit that campaign, for they would give no quarter: This was in the mouths of most whom I heard speak on the subject, officer as well as soldier. I wished at that time my countrymen knew as well as I did, what a murdering and cruel enemy they had to deal with; but experience has since taught this country, what they are to expect at the hands of Britons when in their power.

The prisoners who had been sent on board different men of war at the cove of Cork, were collected together, and the whole of them put on board the Mercury frigate, captain James Montague, except one of the Canadians, who died on the passage from Ireland, and Peter Noble, who made his escape from the Sphynx man of war in this harbour, and by extraordinary swimming, got safe home to New England, & gave intelligence of the usage of his brother-prisoners. The Mercury set sail from this port for Halifax, about the 20th of May, and Sir Peter Parker was about to sail with the land forces, under the command of gen. Clinton, for the reduction of Charlestown, the capital of South Carolina, and when I heard of his defeat in Halifax, it gave me inexpressible satisfaction.[31]

I now found myself under a worse captain than Symonds; for Montague was loaded with prejudices against every body, and every thing that was not stamped with royalty; and being by nature under-witted, his wrath was heavier than the others, or at least his mind was in no instance liable to be diverted by good sense, humour or bravery, of which Symonds was by turns susceptible. A captain Francis Proctor was added to our number of prisoners when we were first put on board this ship: This gentleman had formerly belonged to the English service. The captain, and in fine all the gentlemen of the ship, were very much incensed against him, and put him in irons without

---

[30] Sir Henry Clinton (1730–1795) was second in command to Sir William Howe in America in 1776.

[31] Admiral Sir Peter Parker (1721–1811) set sail in late May 1776 to attack Charlestown. On 28 June, British forces tried to enter Charlestown Harbor only to see three frigates run aground in the low water. After a ten-hour battle, the rest of the fleet withdrew without landing a man.

the least provocation, and he was continued in this miserable situation about three months. In this passage the prisoners were infected with the scurvy, some more and some less, but most of them severely. The ship's crew was to a great degree troubled with it, and I concluded that it was catching: Several of the crew died of it on their passage. I was weak and feeble in consequence of so long and cruel a captivity, yet had but little of the scurvy.

The purser was again expressly forbid by the captain to let me have any thing out of his store; upon which I went on deck, and in the handsomest manner requested the favour of purchasing a few necessaries of the purser, which was denied me; he further told me, that I should be hanged as soon as I arrived at Halifax. I tried to reason the matter with him, but found him proof against reason; I also held up his honour to view, and his behaviour to me and the prisoners in general, as being derogatory to it, but found his honour impenetrable. I then endeavoured to touch his humanity, but found he had none; for his prepossession of bigotry to his own party, had confirmed him in an opinion, that no humanity was due to unroyalists, but seemed to think that heaven and earth were made merely to gratify the king and his creatures; he uttered considerable unintelligible and grovelling ideas, a little tinctured with monarchy, but stood well to his text of hanging me. He afterwards forbid his surgeon to administer any help to the sick prisoners. I was every night shut down in the cable-tire, with the rest of the prisoners, and we all lived miserable while under his power: But I received some generosity from several of the midshipmen, who in degree alleviated my misery; one of their names was Putrass, the names of the others I do not recollect; but they were obliged to be private in the bestowment of their favour, which was sometimes good wine bitters, and at others a generous drink of grog.

Sometime in the first week of June, we came to anchor at the Hook off New-York, where we remained but three days; in which time governor Tryon,[32] Mr. Kemp, the old attorney general of New-York, and several

---

[32] William Tryon (1729–1788) was colonial governor of North Carolina (1765–1771) and New York (1771–1776). Both governorships were convulsed by frontier agitation (the Regulator movement in North Carolina, the Green Mountain Boys in New York). In 1777 he was commissioned to lead a group of Loyalists ("tories") in a series of vindictive raids upon the Connecticut coast. By 1779, when Allen's *Narrative* was published, Tyron was a hated figure in America.

other perfidious and over-grown tories and land-jobbers, came on board. Tryon viewed me with a stern countenance, as I was walking on the leeward side of the deck with the midshipmen; and he and his companions were walking with the captain and lieutenant on the windward side of the same, but never spoke to me, though it is altogether probable that he thought of the old quarrel between him, the old government of New York, and the Green Mountain Boys: Then they went with the captain into the cabbin, and the same afternoon returned on board a vessel which lay near the Hook, where at that time they took sanctuary from the resentment of their injured country. What passed between the officers of the ship and these visitors I know not; but this I know, that my treatment from the principal officers was more severe afterwards.

We arrived at Halifax not far from the middle of June, where the ship's crew which was infested with the scurvy, were taken on shore, and shallow trenches dug, into which they were put, and partly covered with earth.[33] Indeed every proper measure was taken for their relief: The prisoners were not permitted any sort of medicine, but were put on board a sloop which lay in the harbour, near the town of Halifax, surrounded with several men of war and their tenders, and a guard constantly set over them, night and day. The sloop we had wholly to ourselves, except the guard who occupied the forecastle; here we were cruelly pinched with hunger; it seemed to me that we had not more than one third of the common allowance: We were all seized with violent hunger and faintness; we divided our scanty allowance as exact as possible. I shared the same fate with the rest, and though they offered me more than an even share, I refused to accept it, as it was a time of substantial distress, which in my opinion I ought to partake equally with the rest, and set an example of virtue and fortitude to our little common-wealth.

[33] Scurvy is caused by the lack of vitamin C in the diet. By the middle of the eighteenth century, British physicians, led by James Lind, knew that scurvy was caused by the lack of certain fruits and vegetables in the diet; however, not until 1795 did the Royal Navy provide its sailors with a regular daily allowance of lime juice. In the 1772 edition of his *Treatise on the Scurvy*, Lind noted that some people believed that burying a scorbutic person up to the neck in dirt would effect a cure. Lind tended to accept the reports of the success of the cure, though he did not advocate its use.

I sent letter after letter to capt. Montague, (who still had the care of us) and also to his lieutenant, whose name I cannot call to mind, but could obtain no answer, much less a redress of grievances; and to add to the calamity, near a dozen of the prisoners were dangerously ill of the scurvy. I wrote private letters to the doctors, to procure, if possible, some remedy for the sick, but all in vain. The chief physician came by in a boat so close that the oars touched the sloop we were in, and I uttered my complaint in the genteelest manner to him, but he never so much as turned his head, or made me any answer, though I continued speaking 'till he got out of hearing. Our case then become very deplorable. Still I kept writing to the captain, 'till he ordered the guards, as they told me, not to bring any more letters from me to him.

In the mean time an event happened worth relating: One of the men almost dead of the scurvy, lay by the side of the sloop, and a canoe of Indians coming by, he purchased two quarts of strawberries, and eat them at once, and it almost cured him. The money he gave for them, was all he had in the world. After that we tried every way to procure more of that fruit, reasoning from analogy that they might have the same effect on others infested with the same disease, but could obtain none.

Mean while the doctor's mate of the Mercury came privately on board the prison-sloop, and presented me with a large vial of smart drops,[34] which proved to be good for the scurvy, though vegetables and some other ingredients were requisite for a cure; but the drops gave at least a check to the disease: This was a well-timed exertion of humanity, (but the doctor's name has slipped my mind) and in my opinion was the means of saving the lives of several men.

The guard which was set over us, was by this time touched with the feelings of compassion; and I finally trusted one of them with a letter of complaint to governor Arbuthnot[35] of Halifax, which he found means to communicate, and which had the desired effect; for the governor sent an officer and surgeon on board the prison-ship, to know the truth of the complaint. The officer's name was Russel, who

[34] Probably a decoction made from smartweed or smartgrass (a water-pepper), a plant with medicinal properties.

[35] Marriott Arbuthnot (1711–1794), British admiral, was actually commissioner of the navy at Halifax from 1775 to 1778.

LINK

"The Prisoners . . . were put on board a sloop which lay in the harbour, near The town of Halifax, surrounded with several men of war and their tenders, and a guard constantly set over them, night and day. . . ."

Allen goes on to describe the wretched conditions on this British prison ship. European countries in the eighteenth century usually had cartels, or agreements, outlining parole procedures and prisoner exchange. There was no such cartel between Great Britain and the rebellious Americans. Why should there have been? They were countrymen! As a result, prisoner exchange during the American Revolution was not coordinated, forcing both sides to hold large numbers of prisoners at various times, often in wretched conditions. Burgoyne's troops, for example, who surrendered in October 1777, remained in American hands for more than two years. This helps to explain why Allen remained in captivity so long and why he was moved so often: the British simply were not sure what to do with him.

Because the British actually controlled so little territory in North America after the war began, and because their supply lines and reinforcements were undependable, they often used ships as prisons. The American poet Philip Freneau, who was taken captive by the British as he sailed as a passenger to the Caribbean, wrote an angry poem recounting his experiences aboard the British prison-ship *Scorpion*. It is one of many contemporaneous first-hand accounts describing the treatment of prisoners.

> Remembrance shudders at this scene of fears—
> Still in my view some English brute appears,
> Some base-born Hessian slave walks threat'ning by,
> Some servile Scot with murder in his eye
> Still haunts my sight, as vainly they bemoan
> Rebellions manag'd so unlike their own!
> O may I never feel the poignant pain
> To live subjected to such fiends again,
> Stewards and Mates that hostile Britain bore,
> Cut from the gallows on their native shore;

Their ghastly looks and vengeance-beaming eyes
Still to my view in dismal colors rise—
O may I ne'er review these dire abodes,
These piles for slaughter, floating on the floods. . . .
Hail, dark abode! What can with thee compare—
Heat, sickness, famine, death, and stagnant air—
Pandora's box, from whence all mischief flew,
Here real found, torments mankind anew!—
Swift from the guarded decks we rush'd along,
And vainly sought repose, so vast our throng;
Three hundred wretches here, denied all light,
In crowded mansions pass the infernal night,
Some for a bed their tatter'd vestments join,
And some on chests, and some of floors recline;
Shut from the blessings of the evening air,
Pensive we lay with mingled corpses there,
Meagre and wan, and scorch'd with heat below,
We loom'd like ghosts, ere death had made us so—
How could we else, where heat and hunger join'd
Thus to debase the body and the mind,
Where cruel thirst the parching throat invades,
Dries up the man, and fits him for the shades. . . .

The British Prison Ship (1781), I: 73–86, 99–116

held the rank of lieutenant, and treated me in a friendly and polite manner, and was really angry at the cruel and unmanly usage the prisoners met with; and with the surgeon made a true report of matters to governor Arbuthnot, who either by his order or influence, took us next day from the prison-ship to Halifax gaol, where I first became acquainted with the now honourable James Lovel, Esquire, one of the members of Congress for the state of Massachusett's Bay.[36] The sick were taken to the hospital, and the Canadians who were effective, were employed in the King's works; and when their countrymen

[36] James Lovell (1737–1814) was arrested for spying by the British soon after the Battle of Bunker Hill in June 1775. He was sent as a prisoner to Halifax, where he was finally exchanged for Phillip Skene in the autumn of 1776, as Allen notes below. He did not become a member of Congress until after his exchange, serving as a delegate from 1777 to 1782.

were recovered from the scurvy, and joined them, they all deserted the king's employ, and were not heard of at Halifax, as long as the remainder of the prisoners continued there, which was 'till near the middle of October. We were on board the prison-sloop about six weeks, and were landed at Halifax near the middle of August.—Several of our English American prisoners, who were cured of the scurvy at the hospital, made their escape from thence, and after a long time reached their old habitations.

I had now but thirteen with me of those that were taken in Canada, and remained in gaol (with me) in Halifax, who in addition to those that were imprisoned before, made our number about thirty four, who were all locked up in one common large room, without regard to rank, education, or any other accomplishment, where we continued from the setting to the rising sun; and as sundry of them were infected with the gaol and other distempers, the furniture of this spacious room consisted most principally of excrement tubs. We petitioned for a removal of the sick into the hospitals, but were denied. We remonstrated against the ungenerous usage of being confined with the privates, as being contrary to the laws and customs of nations, and particularly ungrateful in them, in consequence of the gentlemen like usage which the British imprisoned officers met with in America; and thus we wearied ourselves, petitioning and remonstrating but to no purpose at all; for general Massey who commanded at Halifax, was as inflexible as the devil himself, (a fine preparative this for Mr. Lovel, member of the Continental Congress.)

Lieutenant Russel (whom I have mentioned before) came to visit me in prison, and assured me that he had done his utmost to procure my parole for enlargement;[37] *at which a British captain, who was the town-major, expressed compassion for the gentlemen confined in the filthy place, and assured me that he had used his influence to procure their enlargement; his name was near like Ramsey.—Among the prisoners there were five in number, who had a legal claim to a parole, viz. James Lovel, Esq. capt. Francis Proctor, a Mr. Howland, master of a continental armed vessel, a Mr. Taylor, his mate, and myself.*

As to the article of provision, we were well served, much better than in any part of my captivity; and since it was Mr. Lovel's misfortune and mine

[37] Parole is the promise of a prisoner of war upon his faith and honor to fulfill stated conditions, in this case the release from close confinement in exchange for the promise not to flee.

to be prisoners, and in so wretched circumstances, I was happy that we were together, as a mutual support and comfort to each other, and to the unfortunate prisoners with us. Our first attention was the preservation of ourselves and injured little republic; the rest of our time we devoted interchangeably to politics and philosophy, as patience was a needful exercise in so evil a situation, but contentment mean and impracticable.

I had not been in this gaol many days, before a worthy and charitable woman, Mrs. Blacden by name, supplied me with a good dinner of fresh meats every day, with garden fruit, and sometimes with a bottle of wine; notwithstanding which I had not been more than three weeks in this place, before I lost all appetite to the most delicious food by the gaol distemper,[38] as sundry of the prisoners, particularly a sergeant Moore, a man of courage and fidelity: I have several times seen him hold the boatswain of the Solebay frigate, when he attempted to strike him, and laughed him out of conceit of using him as a slave.

A doctor visited the sick, and did the best (as I suppose) he could for them, to no apparent purpose. I grew weaker and weaker, as did the rest. Several of them could not help themselves. At last I reasoned in my own mind, that raw onion would be good: I made use of it, and found immediate relief by it, as did the sick in general, particularly sergeant Moore, who it recovered almost from the shades; though I had met with a little revival, still I found the malignant hand of Britain had greatly reduced my constitution with stroke upon stroke. Esquire Lovel and myself used every argument and entreaty that could be well conceived of, in order to obtain gentleman like usage, to no purpose. I then wrote general Massey as severe a letter as I possibly could, with my friend Lovel's assistance: The contents of it was to give the British, as a nation, and him as an individual, their true character: This roused the rascal, for he could not bear to see his and the nation's deformity in that transparent letter, which I sent him; he therefore put himself in a great rage about it, and shewed the letter to a number of British officers, particularly to capt. Smith of the Lark frigate, who instead of joining with him in disapprobation, commended the spirit of it; upon which general Massey said to him, do you take the part of a rebel against me? Captain Smith answered, that he rather spoke his sentiments, and there was a dissention in an opinion between them. Some officers took the part of the general, and others

---

[38] Typhus, which would have been transmitted in eighteenth-century jails through body lice.

of the captain: This I was informed of by a gentleman who had it from captain Smith.

In a few days after this the prisoners were ordered to go on board of a man of war, which was bound for New York; but two of them were not able to go on board, and were left at Halifax; one died, and the other recovered. This was about the 12th of October, and soon after we had got on board, the captain sent for me in particular to come on the quarter deck: I went, not knowing that it was captain Smith, or his ship at that time, and expected to meet the same rigorous usage I had commonly met with, and prepared my mind accordingly; but when I came on deck, the captain met me with his hand, welcomed me to his ship, invited me to dine with him that day, and assured me that I should be treated as a gentleman, and that he had given orders, that I should be treated with respect by the ship's crew. This was so unexpected and sudden a transition, that it drew tears from my eyes, (which all the ill usage I had before met with, was not able to produce) nor could I at first hardly speak, but soon recovered myself, and expressed my gratitude for so unexpected a favour; and let him know, that I felt anxiety of mind in reflecting that his situation and mine was such, that it was not probable that it would ever be in my power to return the favour. Capt. Smith replied, that he had no reward in view, but only treated me as a gentleman ought to be treated; he said this is a mutable world, and one gentleman never knows but that it may be in his power to help another. Soon after I found this to be the same capt. Smith, who (I was told) took my part against general Massey; but he never mentioned any thing of it to me, and I thought it impolite in me to interrogate him as to any disputes which might have arisen between him and the general, on my account, as I was a prisoner, and that it was at his option to make free with me on that subject, if he pleased; and if he did not, I might take it for granted that it would be unpleasing for me to query about it, though I had a strong propensity to converse with him on that subject.

I dined with the captain agreeable to his invitation, and oftentimes with the lieutenants in the gun room, but in general eat and drank with my friend Lovel, and the other gentlemen, who were prisoners with me, where I also slept.

We had a little birth enclosed with canvas, between decks, where we enjoyed ourselves very well, in hopes of an exchange; besides our friends at Halifax had a little notice of our departure, and supplied us with spirituous liquor, and many articles of provision for the coast. Captain Burk having been taken prisoner, was added to our company, (he had commanded an American armed vessel) and was generously treated by the captain, and all the officers of

*the ship, as well as myself. We now had in all near thirty prisoners on board,
and as we were sailing along the coast, (if I recollect right) off Rhode Island,
captain Burk with an under officer of the ship, (whose name I do not recollect)
came to our little birth, proposed to kill captain Smith and the principal officers
of the frigate, and take it; adding that there was thirty five thousand pounds
sterling in the same. Capt. Burk likewise averred, that a strong party out of the
ship's crew, was in the conspiracy, and urged me and the gentlemen that was
with me, to use our influence with the private prisoners, to execute the design,
and take the ship with the cash into one of our own ports.*

*Upon which I replied, that we had been too well used on board to murder the
officers; that I could by no means reconcile it to my conscience, and that in
fact it should not be done; and while I was yet speaking, my friend Lovel confirmed what I had said, and further pointed out the ungratefulness of such
an act; that it did not fall short of murder, and in fine all the gentlemen in
the birth, opposed capt. Burk and his colleague: But they strenuously urged
that the conspiracy would be found out, and that, it would cost them their
lives, provided they did not execute their design. I then interposed spiritedly,
and put an end to further arguments on the subject, and told them that they
might depend upon it upon my honour, that I would faithfully guard captain
Smith's life: if they should attempt the assault, I would assist him, (for they
desired me to remain neuter) and that the same honour that guarded captain
Smith's life, would also guard theirs; and it was agreed by those present not
to reveal the conspiracy, to the intent that no man should be put to death, in
consequence of what had been projected; and captain Burk and his colleague
went to stifle the matter among their associates. I could not help calling to
mind what Captain Smith said to me, when I first came on board:* "This is
a mutable world, and one gentleman never knows but that it may be
in his power to help another."—*Captain Smith and his officers still
behaved with their usual courtesy, and I never heard any more of the conspiracy.*

We arrived before New York, and cast anchor the latter part of
October, where we remained several days, and where capt. Smith
informed me, that he had recommended me to admiral Howe and
general Sir William Howe, as a gentleman of honour and veracity,
and desired that I might be treated as such. Captain Burk was then
ordered on board a prison-ship in the harbour. I took my leave of capt.
Smith, and with the other prisoners was sent on board a transport-ship,
which lay in the harbour, commanded by capt. Craig, who took me

LINK

"This was so unexpected and sudden a transition, that it drew tears from my eyes, (which all the ill usage I had before met with, was not able to produce) nor could I at first hardly speak. . . ."

Sentimentality in our time has become an affected or exaggerated state of mind, one that we view with suspicion. Sentimentality is sappy. Not so in the second half of the eighteenth century, when a sudden surge of interest in the sentimental, or in sensibility, swept England. Manliness at that time connoted not the resistance to tears, feelings, and emotions, as it has at times in our world, but the acceptance and even cultivation of them. Laurence Sterne, in his wildly popular *A Sentimental Journey* (1768), had his narrator, Mr. Yorick, write

> Yes—and then—Ye whose clay-cold heads and lukewarm hearts can argue down or mask your passions, tell me, what trespass is it that man should have [feelings]? Or how his spirit stands answerable to the father of spirits, but for his conduct under them?
>
> If nature has so wove her web of kindness, that some threads of love and desire are entangled with the piece, must the whole web be rent in drawing them out?—Whip me such stoics, great governor of nature! Said I to myself—Wherever thy providence shall place me for the trials of my virtue—whatever is my danger— whatever is my situation—let me feel the movements which rise out of it, and which belong to me as a man, and if I govern them as a good one, I will trust the issues to thy justice—for thou hast made us, and not we ourselves.

In his 12 October 1786 letter to Maria Cosway, Thomas Jefferson composed a dialogue between his "head" (reason) and his "heart" (sensibility, emotions). In it, the head advises the heart to live alone because to form connections with other people leads only to sadness and loss. The heart responds:

> And what more sublime delight than to mingle tears with one whom the hand of heaven hath smitten! To watch over the bed of sickness, & to beguile its tedious & its painful moments! To share our bread with one to whom misfortune has left none! This world abounds indeed with misery: to lighten [its] burthen we must divide it with one another. . . . Had [cold-hearted people] ever felt the solid pleasure of one generous spasm of the heart, they would exchange for it all the frigid speculations of their lives. . . .

> Sensibility is "wove" into the human body, as Sterne has it; it is
> a "spasm" of the heart, as Jefferson puts it. It is an involuntary
> reaction that only "sensible" people can feel and respond to.

into the cabbin with him and his lieutenant: I fared as they did, and
was in every respect well treated in consequence of directions from
captain Smith.

In a few weeks after this I had the happiness to part with my
friend Lovel, (for his sake, who the enemy affected to treat as a private; he was a gentleman of merit, and liberally educated, but had no
commission; they maligned him on account of his unshaken attachment to the cause of his country). He was exchanged for a governor
Phillip Skene of the British.[39] I was continued on board this ship, 'till
the latter part of November, where I contracted an acquaintance with
a captain of the British, (his name has slipped my memory). He was
what we may call a genteel, hearty fellow. I remember an expression
of his over a bottle of wine, to this import: "That there is greatness of
soul for personal friendship to subsist between you and me, as we are
upon opposite sides, and may at another day be obliged to face each
other in the field." (I am confident that he was as faithful as any officer
in the British army.) At another sitting he offered to bet a dozen of
wine, that fort Washington would be in the hands of the British in
three days. I stood the bet, (and would had I known that that would
have been the case) and the third day afterwards we heard a prodigious
heavy cannonade, and that day the fort was taken sure enough.[40]
Some months after, (when I was on parole) he called upon me with
his usual humour, and mentioned the bet. I acknowledged I had lost
it, but he said he did not mean to take it then, as I was a prisoner; that
he would another day call on me, when their army came to Bennington.

---

[39] Phillip Skene (1720–1810) took an active interest in the colonization of present-
day Vermont in the early 1770s. He was authorized by the British to raise a
regiment in 1776, was arrested in Philadelphia while trying to do so, and was
imprisoned in Connecticut until his exchange. His title in 1776 was Lieutenant
Governor of Ticonderoga and Crown Point. He later served under Burgoyne
until the latter's surrender.

[40] Forts Washington and Lee, guarding the North River just north of North
York City, fell to the British after a three-day battle on 18 November 1776.

I replied that he was quite too generous, as I had fairly lost it; besides the Green Mountain Boys would not suffer them to come to Bennington. This was all in good humour. I should have been glad to have seen him after the defeat at Bennington, but did not.

It was customary for the guard to attend the prisoners, which was often changed. One was composed of tories from Connecticut, in the vicinity of Fairfield and Green Farms. The sergeant's name was Hoit. They were very full of their invectives against the country, swaggered of their loyalty to their king, and exclaimed bitterly against the "cowardly Yankies," (as they were pleased to call them) but finally contented themselves with saying, that when the country was overcome, they should be well rewarded for their loyalty, out of the estates of the whigs, which would be confiscated. This I found to be the general language of tories, after I arrived from England on the American coast. I heard sundry of them relate, that the British generals had engaged them an ample reward for all their losses, disappointments and expenditures, out of the forfeited rebels estates.

This language early taught me what to do with tories estates, as far as my influence can go. For it is really a game of hazard between whig and tory: The whigs must inevitably have lost all, in consequence of the abilities of the tories, and their good friends the British; and it is no more than right the tories should run the same risque, in consequence of the abilities of the whigs: But of this more will be observed in the sequel of this narrative.

Some of the last days of November, the prisoners were landed at New York, and I was admitted to parole with the other officers, viz. Proctor, Howland, and Taylor. The privates were put into the filthy churches in New York, with the distressed prisoners that were taken at fort Washington; and the second night sergeant Roger Moore (who was bold and enterprizing) found means to make his escape with every of the remaining prisoners that were taken with me, except three who were soon after exchanged: So that out of thirty one prisoners, who went with me the round exhibited in these sheets, two only died with the enemy, and three only exchanged; one of whom died after he came within our lines; all the rest at different times, made their escape from the enemy.

I now found myself on parole, and restricted to the limits of the city of New-York, where I soon projected means to live in some measure agreeable to my rank, though I was destitute of cash. My constitution was almost worn out by such a long and barbarous captivity. The enemy gave out that I was crazy, and wholly unmanned, but my vitals held sound, (nor was I delirious any more than I have been from my youth up; but my extreme circumstances at certain times, rendered it political to act in some measure the madman) and in consequence of a regular diet and exercise, my blood recruited, and my nerves in great measure recovered their former tone, strength and usefulness, in the course of six months.

I next invite the reader to a retrospect sight and consideration of the doleful scene of inhumanity exercised by general Sir William Howe, and the army under his command, towards the prisoners taken on Long Island, on the twenty seventh day of August, 1776; sundry of whom were in an inhuman and barbarous manner, murdered after they had surrendered their arms; particularly a gen. Odel, (or Woodhul) of the militia, who was hacked to pieces with cutlasses (when alive) by the light horsemen, and a captain Fellows, of the continental army, who was thrust through with a bayonet, of which wound he died instantly.

Sundry others were hanged up by the neck 'till they were dead; five on the limb of a white oak tree, and without any reason assigned, (except that they were fighting in defence of the only blessing worth preserving:) And indeed those who had the misfortune to fall into their hands at fort Washington, in the month of November following, met with but very little better usage, except that they were reserved from immediate death to famish and die with hunger; in fine the word rebel applied to any vanquished persons, without regard to rank, who were in the continental service, on the 27th of August aforesaid, was thought (by the enemy) sufficient to sanctify whatever cruelties they were pleased to inflict, death itself not excepted; but to pass over particulars which would swell my narrative far beyond my design.

The private soldiers who were brought to New York, were crowded into churches, and environed with slavish Hessian guards, a people of a strange language, who were sent to America for no other design but cruelty and desolation; and at others, by merciless Britons, whose mode of communicating ideas being intelligible in this country, served only to tantalize and insult the helpless and perishing; but above all the hellish delight and triumph of the tories over them, as they were dying by hundreds: This was too much for me to bear as a spectator; for I saw the tories exulting over the dead bodies of their murdered countrymen. I have gone into the churches, and seen sundry of the prisoners in the agonies of death, in consequence of very hunger, and others speechless and near death, biting pieces of chips; others pleading for God's sake, for something to eat, and at the same time shivering with the cold. Hollow groans saluted my ears, and despair seemed to be imprinted on every of their countenances. The filth in these churches (in consequence of the fluxes) was almost beyond description. The floors were covered with excrements. I have carefully sought to direct my steps so as to avoid it, but could not. They would beg for God's sake for one copper, or morsel of bread. I have seen in one of these churches seven dead at the same time, lying among the excrements of their bodies.

It was a common practice with the enemy, to convey the dead from these filthy places, in carts, to be slightly buried, and I have seen whole gangs of tories making derision, and exulting over the dead, saying there goes another load of damned rebels. I have observed the British soldiers to be full of their blackguard jokes, and vaunting on these occasions, but they appeared to me less malignant than tories.

The provision dealt out to the prisoners was by no means sufficient for the support of life: It was deficient in quantity, and much more so in quality. The prisoners often presented me with a sample of their bread, which I certify was damaged to that degree, that it was loathsome and unfit to be eaten, and I am bold to aver it, (as my opinion) that it had been condemned, and was of the very worst sort. I have seen and been fed upon damaged bread, (in the course of my captivity) and observed the quality of such bread as has been condemned by the enemy, among which was very little so effectually spoiled as what was dealt out to these prisoners—Their allowance of meat (as they told me) was quite trifling, and of the basest sort. I never saw any of it, but was informed (bad as it was) it was swallowed almost as quick as they got hold of it. I saw some of them sucking bones after they were speechless; others who could yet speak, and had the use of their reason, urged me in the strongest and most pathetic manner, to use my interest in their behalf, for you plainly see (say they) that we are devoted to death and destruction; and after I had examined more particularly into their truly deplorable condition, and had become more fully apprised of the essential facts, I was per-suaded that it was a premeditated and systematical plan of the British

LINK

"The private soldiers who were brought to New York, were crowded into churches, and environed with slavish Hessian guards. . . .they were dying by the hundreds. . . ."

In 1811 Alexander Graydon, who had been a captain in the Continental Army and who had been taken captive at the British victory at Fort Washington, published his *Memoirs*. In them, he too described the conditions in the New York prisons:

> But, while from the advantage of bearing commissions, we had the benefit of free air and the use of our limbs, our poor devoted soldiers were enclosed within walls, scantily supplied with provisions of bad quality, wretchedly clothed, and destitute of sufficient fuel, if indeed they had any. Disease was the inevitable consequence of such a situation; and their prisons, of course, soon became hospitals. A fatal malady was generated; and the mortality, to every heart not steeled by the spirit of party, was truly deplorable. I once, and once only, ventured to penetrate into these abodes of human misery and despair. But to what purpose repeat my visit, when I had neither relief to administer, nor comfort to bestow! What could I say to the unhappy victims who appealed to me for assistance, or sought my advice as to the alternative of death or apostacy? . . .

Graydon reveals not just the wretched conditions for the captured soldiers, but also the fact that conditions were different for officers and enlisted men. Graydon and Allen did not have an easy time of it, but neither did they have it as bad as did the enlisted men.

Jabez Fitch, an officer who had been taken captive at the Battle of Long Island in August 1776, wrote in his *Narrative* that by December 1776,

> Most of the [officers] who were now Prisoners, were Endulg'd with Liberty to walk the Streets &c within the Bounds of the City, from sunrise to sunset; which Endulgence was continued as long as we Remain'd in the City; Nor was this Enlargement at all Disagreable, as we had suffered almost three months in close Imprisonment, great part of which time, we had been in the most disagreable Situation. . . . Having obtain'd the [aforesaid] Endulgence, the first Objects of our Attention, were the poor men who had been unhappily Captivated with us; they had been landed about the same Time that we were, & confin'd in several Churches & other large Buildings; And alth'o we had often [received] Inteligence from them, with the most deplorable Representation of their miserable sitiuation, yet when we

> came to Visit them, we found their sufferings vastly superior to what
> we had been able to Conceive, nor are words sufficient to convey an
> Adequate Idea of their Unparrallal'd Calamity. . . .

council, to destroy the youths of our land, with a view thereby to
deter the country, and make it submit to their despotism; but that I
could not do them any material service, and that by any public
attempt for that purpose, I might endanger myself by frequenting places
the most nauseous and contagious that could be conceived of. I refrained
going into the churches, but frequently conversed with such of the
prisoners as were admitted to come out into the yard, and found that
the systematical usage still continued. The guard would often drive
me away with their fixed bayonets. A Hessian (one day) followed me five
or six rods, but by making use of my legs, got rid of the lubber. Sometimes
I could obtain a little conversation, notwithstanding their severities.

I was in one of the church yards, and it was rumoured among
those in the church, and sundry of the prisoners came with their
usual complaints to me, and among the rest a large boned tall young
man, (as he told me from Pennsylvania) who was reduced to a mere
skeleton; said he was glad to see me, before he died, which he had
expected to have done last night, but was a little revived; he furthermore informed me, that he and his brother had been urged to enlist
into the British, but had both resolved to die first; that his brother had
died last night, in consequence of that resolution, and that he
expected shortly to follow him; but I made the other prisoners stand
a little off, and told him with a low voice to list; he then asked,
whether it was right in the sight of God? I assured him that it was,
and that duty to himself obliged him to deceive the British by enlisting,
and deserting the first opportunity; upon which he answered with
transport, that he would list. I charged him not to mention my name
as his adviser, lest it should get air, and I should be closely confined,
in consequence of it.

The integrity of these suffering prisoners is hardly credible. Many
hundreds, I am confident, submitted to death, rather than enlist into
the British service, which (I am informed) they most generally were
pressed to do. I was astonished at the resolution of the two brothers particularly; it seems that they could not be stimulated to such exertions of
heroism from ambition, as they were but obscure soldiers; strong
indeed must the internal principle of virtue be, which supported

them to brave death, and one of them went thro' the operation, as did many hundred others. I readily grant that instances of public virtue are no excitement to the sordid and vicious, nor on the other hand, will all the barbarity of Britain and Heshland awaken them to a sense of their duty to the public; but these things will have their proper effect on the generous and brave.

The officers on parole were most of them zealous, if possible, to afford the miserable soldiery relief, and often consulted with one another on the subject, but to no effect, being destitute of the means of subsistance, which they needed; nor could the officers project any measure, which they thought would alter their fate, or so much as be a means of getting them out of those filthy places to the privilege of fresh air. Some projected that all the officers should go in procession to general Howe, and plead the cause of the perishing soldiers; but this proposal was negatived for the following reasons, viz. because that general Howe must needs be well acquainted and have a thorough knowledge of the state and condition of the prisoners in every of their wretched apartments, and that much more particular and exact than any officer on parole could be supposed to have, as the general had a return of the circumstances of the prisoners, by his own officers every morning, of the number which were alive, as also the number which died every twenty four hours, and consequently the bill of mortality, as collected from the daily returns, lay before him with all the material situations and circumstances of the prisoners; and provided the officers should go in procession to general Howe, according to the projection, it would give him the greatest affront, and that he would either retort upon them; that it was no part of their parole to instruct him in his conduct to prisoners; that they were mutinying against his authority, and by affronting him, had forfeited their parole; or that more probably, instead of saying one word to them, would order them all into as wretched a confinement as the soldiers whom they sought to relieve; for at that time, the British, from the general to the private centinel, were in full confidence, nor did they so much as hesitate but that they should conquer the country. Thus the consultation of the officers was confounded and broken to pieces, in consequence of the dread, which at that time lay on their minds, of offending general Howe; for they conceived so murderous a tyrant would not be too good to destroy even the officers, on the least pretence of an affront, as they were equally

in his power with the soldiers; and as general Howe perfectly understood the condition of the private soldiers, it was argued that it was
exactly such as he and his council had devised, and as he meant to
destroy them, it would be to no purpose for them to try to dissuade
him from it, as they were helpless and liable to the same fate, on giving
the least affront; indeed anxious apprehensions disturbed them in
their then circumstances.

Mean time mortality raged to such an intolerable degree among
the prisoners, that the very school boys in the streets knew the mental
design of it in some measure; at least they knew that they were
starved to death. Some poor women contributed to their necessity,
'till their children were almost starved, and all persons of common
understanding knew that they were devoted to the cruellest and
worst of deaths. It was also proposed by some to make a written representation of the condition of the soldiery, and the officers to sign it;
and that it should be couched in such terms, as though they were
apprehensive that the general was imposed upon by his officers, in
their daily returns to him of the state and condition of the prisoners;
and that therefore the officers moved with compassion, were con-
strained to communicate to him the facts relative to them, nothing
doubting but that they would meet with a speedy redress; but this
proposal was most generally negatived also, and for much the same
reason offered in the other case; for it was conjectured that general
Howe's indignation would be moved against such officers as should
attempt to whip him over his officers backs; that he would discern
that himself was really struck at, and not the officers who made the
daily returns; and therefore self-preservation deterred the officers
from either petitioning or remonstrating to general Howe, either ver-
bally or in writing; as also the consideration that no valuable purpose
to the distressed would be obtained.

I made several rough drafts on the subject, one of which I exhibited
to the colonels Magaw, Miles and Atlee, and they said that they
would consider the matter; soon after I called on them, and some of
the gentlemen informed me, that they had wrote to the general on the
subject, and I concluded, that the gentlemen thought it best that they
should write without me, as there was such spirited aversion sub-
sisting between the British and me.

In the mean time a col. Hussecker, of the continental army, (as he
then reported) was taken prisoner, and brought to New-York, who

gave out that the country was most universally submitting to the English king's authority, and that there would be little or no more opposition to Great Britain: This at first gave the officers a little shock, but in a few days they recovered themselves; for this colonel Hussecker being a German, was feasting with general De Heister, his countryman, and from his conduct they were apprehensive, that he was a knave; at least he was esteemed so by most of the officers; it was nevertheless a day of trouble. The enemy blasphemed. Our little army was retreating in New Jersey, and our young men murdered by hundreds in New York: The army of Britain and Heshland prevailed for a little season, as though it was ordered by Heaven to shew to the latest posterity, what the British would have done, if they could, and what the general calamity must have been, in consequence of their conquering the country, and to excite every honest man to stand forth in the defence of liberty, and to establish the independency of the United States of America for ever: But this scene of adverse fortune did not discourage a Washington: The illustrious American hero remained immovable. In liberty's cause he took up his sword: This reflection was his support and consolation in the day of his humiliation, when he retreated before the enemy, through New Jersey into Pennsylvania. Their triumph only roused his indignation, and the important cause of his country, which lay near his heart, moved him to cross the Delaware again, and take ample satisfaction on his pursuers. No sooner had he circumvallated his haughty foes and appeared in *terrible array*, but the host of Heshland fell. This taught America the intrinsic worth of perseverance, and the generous sons of freedom flew to the standard of their common safeguard and defence; from which time the arm of American liberty hath prevailed.

This surprize and capture of the Hessians enraged the enemy, who were still vastly more numerous than the continental troops: They therefore collected, and marched from Princeton, to attack general Washington, who was then at Trenton, having previously left a detachment from their main body at Princeton, for the support of that place. This was a trying time, for our worthy General (tho' in possession of a late most astonishing victory) was by no means able to withstand the collective force of the enemy; but his sagacity soon suggested a stratagem to effect that which by force to him was at that time impracticable: He therefore amused the enemy with a number of fires, and in the night made a forced march, undiscovered by them,

LINK

". . . . the very boys in the streets knew the mental design of it in some measure. . . ."

Allen, like many of the founding fathers, was, in a sense, paranoid. They believed that all events had discernible causes, and that therefore effects that *felt* like the hand of tyranny—effects like taxation without representation and poor care for prisoners—had to be the result of tyrannous intentions. In an article entitled "Conspiracy and the Paranoid Style: Causality and Deceit in the Eighteenth Century," the historian Gordon Wood writes that "this conspiratorial mode of explanation represented an enlightened stage in Western man's long struggle to comprehend his social reality. It flowed from the scientific promise of the Enlightenment and represented an effort, perhaps in retrospect a last desperate effort, to hold men personally and morally responsible for their actions." This is what Allen means by "mental design": his British captors *intended* for their American prisoners to suffer. Looking back on events from our point of view, we can see that the "real" cause of suffering for American prisoners was neglect and an ineffective bureaucracy.

Nowhere is the conspiratorial, paranoid style better seen than in the Declaration of Independence. Jefferson's draft insists, for example, that "when a long train of abuses & usurpations begun at a distinguished period and pursuing invariably the same object, envinces a design to reduce [the people] under absolute despotism, it is their right, it is their duty to throw off such a government." What follows then is his long list of "facts . . . submitted to a candid world," each of which begins with a direct reference to the king: "He has refused assent to laws . . . . He has forbidden his governors . . . . He has refused to pass other laws," etc. In point of fact, "he," the king of England, simply did not have the independent agency to act in the way that Jefferson suggests he did. But that did not stop Jefferson and Allen from thinking that he did. Thus, as Allen notes at the beginning of his *Narrative*, events at Lexington in April 1775 envinced a "systematical . . . attempt . . . to enslave America." Someone had to be responsible for the North American policy, and at various times the founding fathers thought they knew: George III, or Parliament, or William Howe. *Someone.*

and the next morning fell in with their rear guard at Princeton, and killed and took most of them prisoners. The main body too late perceiving their rear was attacked, hurried back with all speed, but to their mortification found they were out generalled, and baffled by general Washington, who was retired with his little army towards Morristown, and was out of their power. These repeated successes, one on the back of the other, chagrined the enemy prodigiously, and had an amazing operation in the scale of American politics, and undoubtedly was one of the corner-stones, on which their fair structure of independency has been fabricated; for the country at no one time has ever been so much dispirited as just before the morning of this glorious success, which in part dispelled the gloomy clouds of oppression and slavery, which lay pending over America, big with the ruin of this and future generations, and enlightened and spirited her sons to redouble their blows on a merciless and haughty, and (I may add) perfidious enemy.[41]

Furthermore this success had a mighty effect on general Howe and his council, and roused them to a sense of their own weakness, and convinced them that they were neither omniscient or omnipotent. Their obduracy and death-designing malevolence in some measure, abated or was suspended. The prisoners who were condemned to the most wretched and cruellest of deaths, and who survived to this period, (though most of them died before) were immediately ordered to be sent within general Washington's lines for an exchange, and in consequence of it, were taken out of their filthy and poisonous places of confinement, and sent out of New York to their friends in haste; several of them fell dead in the streets of New York, as they attempted to walk to the vessels in the harbour, for their intended embarkation.—What numbers lived to reach the lines I cannot ascertain, but from concurrent representations which I have since received from numbers of people who lived in and adjacent to such parts of the country, where they were received from the enemy, I apprehend that

---

[41] Allen's outline here is correct. After severe defeats at Long Island in August, New York in September and October, and Forts Washington and Lee in November, Washington retreated with his army across New Jersey in December 1776. He recrossed the Delaware River in New Jersey on Christmas night and defeated celebrating Hessians at Trenton on December 26 and a British garrison at Princeton on January 3.

most of them died in consequence of the vile usage of the enemy. Some who were eye-witnesses of that scene of mortality, (more especially in that part which continued after the exchange took place) are of opinion, that it was partly in consequence of a slow poison; but this I refer to the doctors that attended them, who are certainly the best judges.

Upon the best calculation I have been able to make from personal knowledge, and the many evidences I have collected in support of the facts, I learn that of the prisoners taken on Long Island, fort Washington, and some few others, at different times and places, about two thousand perished with hunger, cold and sickness, (occasioned by the filth of their prisons) at New York, and a number more on their passage to the continental lines; most of the residue who reached their friends, having received their death wound, could not be restored by the assistance of physicians and friends; but like their brother-prisoners, fell a sacrifice to the relentless and scientific barbarity of Britain. I took as much pains as my circumstances would admit of, to inform myself not only of matters of fact, but likewise of the very design and aims of general Howe and his council: The latter of which I predicated on the former, and submit it to the candid public.

And lastly the aforesaid success of the American arms, had a happy effect on the continental officers, who were on parole at New York: A number of us assembled, (but not in a public manner) and with full bowls and glasses, drank general Washington's health, and were not unmindful of Congress and our worthy friends on the continent, and almost forgot that we were prisoners.

A few days after this recreation, a British officer of rank and importance in their army, (whose name I shall not mention in this narrative, for certain reasons, tho' I have mentioned it to some of my close friends and confidents) sent for me to his lodgings, and told me, "That faithfulness (though in a wrong cause) had nevertheless recommended me to general Sir William Howe, who was minded to make me a colonel of a regiment of new levies, (alias tories) in the British service, and proposed that I should go with him, and some other officers, to England, who would embark for that purpose in a few days, and there be introduced to lord G. Germain,[42] and probably to the king; and that

---

[42] Lord George Germaine (1716–1785) was Colonial Secretary in Great Britain, directing military measures in North America.

previously I should be cloathed equal to such an introduction, and instead of paper rags,[43] be paid in hard guineas; after this should embark with general Burgoyne, and assist in the reduction of the country, which infallibly would be conquered, and when that should be done, I should have a large tract of land, whether on the New Hampshire Grants, or in Connecticut; it would make no odds, as the country would be forfeited to the crown." I then replied, "That if by faithfulness I had recommended myself to gen. Howe, I should be loth, by unfaithfulness, to lose the general's good opinion; besides, that I viewed the offer of land to be similar to that which the devil offered Jesus Christ, "To give him all the kingdoms of the world, if he would fall down and worship him;"[44] when at the same time that damned soul had not one foot of land upon the earth." This closed the conversation, and the gentleman turned from me with an air of dislike, saying, that I was a bigot; upon which I retired to my lodgings.

Near the last of November I was admitted to parole in New York, with many other American officers, and on the 22d day of January, 1777, was with them directed by the British commisary of prisoners to be quartered on the westerly part of Long Island, and our parole continued. During my imprisonment there, no occurrences worth observation happened. I obtained the means of living as well as I desired, which in great measure repaired my constitution, which had been greatly injured by the severities of an inhuman captivity. I now began to feel myself composed, expecting either an exchange or continuance in good and honourable treatment; but alas! my visionary expectations soon vanished. The news of the conquest of Ticonderoga by gen. Burgoyne, and the advance of his army into the country, made the haughty Britons again to feel their importance, and with that their insatiable thirst for cruelty.

The private prisoners at New York, and some of the officers on parole, felt the severity of it.—Burgoyne was their toast and demi god: To him they paid adoration: In him the tories placed their confidence, "and forgot the Lord their God," and served Howe, Burgoyne,

---

[43] In the eighteenth century, paper was made from cloth (including old rags), not wood pulp.

[44] "And [the devil] saith unto him, All these things will I give to thee, if thou wilt fall down and worship me" (Matthew 5.9).

and Knyphausen,[45] "and became vile in their own imaginations, and their foolish hearts were darkened, professing" to be great politicians, and relying on foreign and merciless invaders, and with them seeking the ruin, bloodshed and destruction of their country, "became fools," expecting with them to share a dividend in the confiscated estates of their neighbours and countrymen, who fought for the whole country, and the religion and liberties thereof:—"Therefore God gave them over to strong delusions, to believe a lie, that they all might be damned."[46]

The twenty-fifth day of August I was apprehended, and under pretext of artful, mean and pitiful pretences, (that I had infringed on my parole) taken from a tavern, where there were more than a dozen officers present, and in the very place where those officers and myself were directed to be quartered, put under a strong guard, and taken to New York, where I expected to make my defence before the commanding officer; but contrary to my expectations, and without the least solid pretence of justice or a trial, was again encircled with a strong guard with fixed bayonets, and conducted to the provost-gaol in a lonely apartment, next above the dungeon, and was denied all manner of subsistence either by purchase or allowance. The second day I offered a guinea for a meal of victuals, but was denied it, and the third day I offered eight Spanish milled dollars for a like favour, but was again denied, and all that I could get out of the sergeant's mouth, was, that by God he would obey his orders. I now perceived myself to be again in substantial trouble. In this condition I formed an oblique acquaintance with a captain Edward Travis, of Virginia, (who was in the dungeon below me) through a little hole which was cut with a pen-knife, through the floor of my apartment which communicated with the dungeon; it was a small crevice, through which I could discern but a very small part of his face at once, when he plied it to the hole; but from the discovery of him in the situation which we were both then in, I could not have known him, (which I found to be true by an after acquaintance.) I could nevertheless hold a conversation with him, and soon perceived him to be a gentleman of high spirits, who had a high

---

[45] Knyphausen, a Hessian general [Allen's note].

[46] Allen draws in this passage upon the language of Romans 1.16–32, where Paul claims that the wrath of God will be visited upon the ungodly and unrighteous.

sense of honour, and felt as big as though he had been in a palace, and had treasures of wrath in store against the British. In fine I was charmed with the spirit of the man; he had been near or quite four months in that dungeon, with murderers, thieves, and every species of criminals, and all for the sole crime of unshaken fidelity to his country; but his spirits were above dejection, and his mind unconquerable. I engaged to do him every service in my power, and in a few weeks afterwards, with the united petitions of the officers in the provost, procured his dismission from the dark mansion of fiends to the apartments of his petitioners.

And it came to pass on the third day, at the going down of the sun, that I was presented with a piece of boiled pork, and some biscuit, which the sergeant gave me to understand, was my allowance, and I fed sweetly on the same; but I indulged my appetite by degrees, and in a few days more, was taken from that apartment, and conducted to the next loft or story, where there were above twenty continental and some militia officers, who had been taken and imprisoned there, besides some private gentlemen who had been dragged from their own homes to that filthy place, by tories. Several of every of the denominations mentioned died there, some before, and others after I was put there.

The history of the proceedings relative to the provost only, was I particular, would swell a volume larger than this whole narrative: Shall therefore only notice such of the occurrences which are most extraordinary.[47]

Capt. Vandyke bore with an uncommon fortitude near twenty months confinement in this place, and in the mean time was very serviceable to others who were confined with him. The allegation against him, as the cause of his confinement, was very extraordinary: He was accused of setting fire to the city of New York, (at the time the west part of it was consumed)[48] when it was a known fact, that he had been in the provost a week before the fire broke out; and in like manner, frivolous were the ostensible accusations against most of those who were there confined; the case of two militia officers excepted, who were taken in

---

[47] I have not attempted to identify all the men whom Allen mentions in the next several paragraphs.

[48] Soon after the British army occupied New York City in the fall of 1776, a fire broke out and destroyed about a thousand homes. The cause of the fire was never determined.

their attempting to escape from their parole; and probably there may be some other instances which might justify such a confinement.

Mr. William Miller, a committee-man,[49] from West Chester county, and state of New York, was taken from his bed in the dead of night, by his tory neighbours, and was starved for three days and nights in a department of the same gaol; add to this the denial of fire, and that in a cold season of the year, in which time he walked day and night, to defend himself against the frost, and when he complained of such a reprehensible conduct, the word rebel or committee-man was deemed by the enemy a sufficient atonement for any inhumanity that they could invent or inflict. He was a man of good natural understanding, a close and sincere friend to the liberties of America, and endured fourteen months cruel imprisonment with that magnanimity of soul, which reflects honour on himself and country.

Major Levi Wells and captain Ozias Bissel were apprehended and taken under guard from their parole on Long Island, to the provost, on as fallacious pretences as the former, and were there continued 'till their exchange took place, which was near five months. Their fidelity and zealous attachment to their country's cause, which was more than commonly conspicuous, was undoubtedly the real cause of their confinement.

Major Brinton Payne, captain Flahaven, and captain Randolph, who had at different times distinguished themselves by their bravery, especially at the several actions in which they were taken, was all the provocation they gave, for which they suffered about a years confinement each in the same filthy gaol.

A few weeks after my confinement, on the like fallacious and wicked pretences, was brought to the same place, from his parole on Long Island, major Otho Holland Williams, (now a full colonel in the continental army). In his character are united the gentleman, officer, soldier and friend; he walked through the prison with an air of great disdain; said he, "Is this the treatment which gentlemen of the continental army are to expect from the rascally British, when in their power? Heavens forbid it!" He was continued there about five months, and then exchanged for a British major.

---

[49] A reference to either the Committees of Correspondence or the Committees of Inspection, extralegal associations of patriots in each colony that tried to organize resistance to the British in the years leading up to the Declaration of Independence.

John Fell, Esq;[50] (now a member of Congress for the state of New Jersey) was taken from his own house by a gang of infamous tories, and by order of a British general, was sent to the provost, where he was continued near one year. The stench of the gaol, which was very loathsome and unhealthy, occasioned a hoarseness of the lungs, which proved fatal to many who were there confined, and reduced this gentleman near to the point of death; he was indeed given over by his friends who were about him, and himself concluded that he must die. I could not endure the thought that so worthy a friend to America should have his life stole from him in such a mean, base, and scandalous a manner, and that his family and friends should be bereaved of so great and desirable a blessing, as his further care, usefulness and examples, might prove to them. I therefore wrote a letter to gen. Robertson, (who commanded in town) and being touched with the most sensible feelings of humanity which dictated my pen to paint dying distress in such lively colours that it wrought conviction even on the obduracy of a British general, and produced his order to remove the now honourable John Fell, Esq; out of gaol, to private lodgings in town; in consequence of which he slowly recovered his health. There is so extraordinary a circumstance which intervened, concerning this letter, that it is worth noticing.

Previous to the sending it, I exhibited the same to the gentlemen on whose behalf it was wrote, for his approbation, and he forbid me to send it in the most positive and explicit terms; his reason was, "That the enemy knew by every morning's report, the condition of all the prisoners, mine in particular, as I have been gradually coming to my end for a considerable time, and they very well knew it, and likewise determined it should be accomplished, as they had served many others; that to ask a favour, would give the merciless enemy occasion to triumph over me in my last moments, and therefore I will ask no favours from them, but resign myself to my supposed fate." But the letter I sent without his knowledge, and I confess I had but little expectations from it, yet could not be easy 'till I had sent it. It may be worth a remark, that this gentleman was an Englishman born, and

---

[50] John Fell was indeed taken from his home by Loyalist raiders on 22 April 1776 and was not released until 11 May 1778. Later that year, he was elected to Congress, where he served for two years.

from the beginning of the revolution, has invariably asserted, and maintained the cause of liberty.

The British have made so extensive an improvement of the provost during the present revolution 'till of late, that a very short definition will be sufficient for the dullest apprehensions. It may be with propriety called the British inquisition, and calculated to support their oppressive measures and designs, by suppressing the spirit of liberty; as also a place to confine the criminals, and most infamous wretches of their own army, where many gentlemen of the American army, and citizens thereof, were promiscuously confined, with every species of criminals; but they divided into different apartments, and kept at as great a remove as circumstances permitted, but it was nevertheless at the option of a villainous sergeant who had the charge of the provost, to take any gentleman from their room, and put them into the dungeon, which was often the case: At two different times I was taken down stairs for that purpose, by a file of soldiers with fixed bayonets, and the sergeant brandishing his sword at the same time, and having been brought to the door of the dungeon, I there flattered the vanity of the sergeant, whose name was Keef, by which means I procured the surprizing favour to return to my companions; but some of the high mettled young gentlemen could not bear his insolence, and determined to keep at a distance, and neither please or displease the villain, but none could keep clear of his abuse; however, mild measures were the best; he did not hesitate to call us damned Rebels, and use us with the coarsest language. The captains Flahaven, Randolph and Mercer, were the objects of his most flagrant and repeated abuses, who were many times taken to the dungeon, and there continued at his pleasure. Captain Flahaven took cold in the dungeon, and was in a declining state of health, but an exchange delivered him, and in all probability saved his life.

It was very mortifying to bear with the insolence of such a vicious and ill-bred imperious rascal. Remonstrances against him were preferred to the commander of the town, but no relief could be obtained, for his superiors were undoubtedly well pleased with his abusive conduct to the gentlemen, under the severities of his power, and remonstrating against his infernal conduct, only served to confirm him in authority, and for this reason I never made any remonstrances on the subject, but only stroaked him, for I knew that he was but a cat's paw in the hands of the British officers, and that if he should use us well, he would immediately be put out of that trust, and a worse man appointed to succeed him; but there was no need of making any new appointment, for Cunningham, their provost marshal, and Keef, his deputy, were as great rascals as their army could boast of, except one Joshua Loring,[51] an infamous tory, who was their commissary of prisoners, nor can any of these be supposed to be equally criminal with general Sir William Howe and his associates, who prescribed and directed the murders and cruelties, which were by them perpetrated.

This Loring is a monster!—There is not his like in human shape. He exhibits a smiling countenance, and on a superficial acquaintance, seems to wear a phiz of humanity, but has been instrumentally capable of the most consummate acts of wickedness, (which were firstly projected by an abandoned British council, cloathed with the authority of a Howe) murdering premeditately (in cool blood) near or quite two thousand helpless prisoners, and that in the most clandestine, mean and shameful manner, (at New York). He is the most mean-spirited, cowardly, deceitful, and destructive animal in God's creation below, and legions of infernal devils, with all their tremendous horrors, are impatiently ready to receive Howe and him, with all their detestable accomplices, into the most exquisite agonies of the hottest region of hell-fire.

The sixth day of July, 1777, general St. Clair, and the army under his command, evacuated Ticonderoga, and retreated with the main body through Hubberdton into Castleton, which was but six miles distance, when his rear-guard commanded by colonel Seth Warner, was attacked at Hubberdton by a body of the enemy of about two thousand commanded by gen. Fraser. Warner's command consisted of his own and two other regiments, viz. Francis's, and Hale's, and some scattering and enfeebled soldiers. His whole number, according to information, was near or quite one thousand; part of which were Green Mountain Boys; about seven hundred out of the whole he brought into action. The enemy advanced boldly, and the two bodies

---

[51] Joshua Loring (1744–1789), born in America to a British naval officer and his American wife, served with the British colonial army and remained loyal when war broke out. He was appointed commissary of prisoners in the British Army in January 1777. Other American leaders complained of his excessive cruelty to and neglect of prisoners.

formed within about sixty yards of each other. Col. Warner having formed his own regiment, and that of col. Francis's, did not wait for the enemy, but gave them a heavy fire from his whole line, and they returned it with great bravery. It was by this time dangerous for those of both parties, who were not prepared for the world to come; but col. Hale being apprised of the danger, never brought his regiment to the charge, but left Warner and Francis to stand the blowing of it, and fled, but luckily fell in with an inconsiderable number of the enemy, and to his eternal shame, surrendered himself a prisoner.

The conflict was very bloody.—Colonel Francis fell in the same, but colonel Warner, and the officers under his command as also the soldiery, behaved with great resolution. The enemy broke, and gave way on the right and left, but formed again, and renewed the attack; in the mean time the British grenadiers, in the center of the enemy's line, maintained the ground, and finally carried it with the point of the bayonet, and Warner retreated with great reluctance. Our loss was about thirty men killed, and that of the enemy amounted to three hundred men killed, including a major Grant. The enemy's loss I learnt from the confession of their own officers, when a prisoner with them. I heard them likewise complain, that the Green Mountain Boys took sight.

The next movement of the enemy, of any material consequence, was their investing Bennington, (with a design to demolish it, and subject its Mountaineers, to whom they had a great aversion) with fifteen hundred chosen men, including tories, with the highest expectation of success, and having chosen an eminence of strong ground, fortified it with slight breast works, and two pieces of cannon; but the government of the young state of Vermont, being previously jealous of such an attempt of the enemy, and in due time had procured a number of brave militia from the government of the state of New Hampshire, who together with the militia of the north part of Berkshire county, and state of Massachusetts, and the Green Mountain Boys, constituted a body of desperadoes, under the command of the intrepid general Stark, who in number were about equal to the enemy.

Colonel Herrick, who commanded the Green Mountain Rangers, and who was second in command, being thoroughly acquainted with the ground where the enemy had fortified, proposed to attack them in their works upon all parts, at the same time. This plan being adopted by the general and his council of war, the little militia brigade of undisciplined heroes, with their long brown firelocks, (the best security of a free people) without either cannon or bayonets, was, on the 16th day of August, led on to the attack by their bold commanders, in the face of the enemy's dreadful fire, (and to the astonishment of the world, and burlesque of discipline) carried every part of their lines in less than one quarter of an hour after the attack became general, took their cannon, killed and captivated more than two thirds of their number, which immortalized genral Stark, and made Bennington famous to posterity.

Among the enemy's slain was found col. Baum, their commander, a col. Pfester, who headed an infamous gang of tories, and a large part of his command; and among the prisoners was Major Meibome, their second in command, a number of British and Hessian officers, surgeons, &c. and more than one hundred of the aforementioned Pfester's command. The prisoners being collected together, were sent to the meeting-house in the town, by a strong guard, and general Stark not imagining any present danger, the militia scattered from him to rest and refresh themselves; in this situation he was on a sudden attacked by a reinforcement of eleven hundred of the enemy, commanded by a governor Skene, with two field pieces: They advanced in regular order, and kept up the incessant fire, especially from their field pieces, and the remaining militia retreating slowly before them, disputed the ground inch by inch. The enemy were heard to halloo to them, saying stop Yankees.

In the mean time col. Warner, with about one hundred and thirty men of his regiment, (who were not in the first action) arrived and attacked the enemy with great fury, (being determined to have ample revenge on account of the quarrel at Hubberdton) which brought them to a stand, and soon after gen. Stark and col. Herrick brought on more of the scattered militia, and the action became general; in a few minutes, the enemy were forced from their cannon, gave way on all parts and fled, and the shouts of victory were a second time proclaimed in favour of the militia. The enemy's loss in killed and prisoners, in these two actions, amounted to more than twelve hundred men, and our loss did not exceed fifty men.

This was a bitter stroke to the enemy, but their pride would not permit them to hesitate but that they could vanquish the country, and as a specimen of their arrogancy, I shall insert gen. Burgoyne's

PROCLAMATION

"By *John Burgoyne,* Esq; lieutenant general of his majesty's armies in America, colonel of the queen's regiment of light dragoons, governor of fort William in North Britain, one of the representatives of the commons of Great Britain in Parliament, and commanding an army and fleet employed on an expedition from Canada, &c. &c. &c.

THE forces entrusted to my command are designed to act in concert, and upon a common principle, with the numerous armies and fleets which already display in every quarter of America, the power, the justice, and when properly sought, the mercy of the king.

The cause in which the British arms are thus exerted, applies to the most affecting interests of the human heart; and the military servants of the crown, at first called forth for the sole purpose of restoring the rights of the constitution, now combine with love of their country, and duty to their sovereign, the other extensive incitements which spring from a due sense of the general privileges of mankind. To the eyes and ears of the temperate part of the public, and to the breasts of suffering thousands in the provinces, be the melancholy appeal, whether the present unnatural rebellion has not been made a foundation for the compleatest system of tyranny that ever God in his displeasure, suffered for a time to be exercised over a froward and stubborn generation.

Arbitrary imprisonment, confiscation of property, persecution and torture, unprecedented in the inquisitions of the Romish church, are among the palpable enormities that verify the affirmative. These are inflicted by assemblies and committees, who dare to profess themselves friends to liberty, upon the most quiet subjects, without distinction of age or sex, for the sole crime, often for the sole suspicion, of having adhered in principal to the government under which they were born, and to which by every tie, divine and human, they owe allegiance. To consummate these shocking proceedings, the profanation of religion is added to the most profligate prostitution of common reason; the consciences of men are set at nought; and multitudes are compelled not only to bear arms, but also to swear subjection to an usurpation they abhor.

Animated by these considerations; at the head of troops in the full powers of health, discipline, and valour; determined to strike where necessary, and anxious to spare where possible, I by these presents invite and exhort all persons, in all places where the progress of this army may point,—and by the blessing of God I will extend it far,—to maintain such a conduct as may justify me in protecting their lands, habitations, and families. The intention of this address is to hold forth security, not depredation to the country.

To those whom spirit and principle may induce to partake the glorious task of redeeming their countrymen from dungeons, and re-establishing the blessings of legal government, I offer encouragement and employment; and upon the first intelligence of their associations, I will find means to assist their undertakings. The domestic, the industrious, the infirm, and even the timid inhabitants, I am desirous to protect, provided they remain quietly at their houses; that they do not suffer their cattle to be removed, nor their corn or forage to be secreted or destroyed; that they do not break up their bridges or roads; nor by any other act, directly or indirectly, endeavour to obstruct the operations of the king's troops, or supply or assist those of the enemy.

Every species of provision brought to my camp, will be paid for at an equitable rate, and in solid coin.

In consciousness of christianity, my royal master's clemency, and the honour of soldiership, I have dwelt upon this invitation, and wished for more persuasive terms to give it impression: And let not people be led to disregard it, by considering their distance from the immediate situation of my camp.—I have but to give stretch to the Indian forces under my direction, and they amount to thousands, to overtake the hardened enemies of Great Britain and America; I consider them the same wherever they may lurk.

If notwithstanding these endeavours, and sincere inclinations to effect them, the phrensy of hostility should remain, I trust I shall stand acquitted in the eyes of God and men, in denouncing and executing the vengeance of the state against the wilful outcasts.—The messengers of justice and of wrath await them in the field; and devastation, famine, and every concomitant horror that a reluctant but indispensable prosecution of military duty must occasion, will bar the way to their return.

Camp near Ticonderoga, 4th July, 1777. *J. Burgoyne.* By order of his excellency the lieutenant general,

Robt. Kingston, secretary.

General Burgoyne was still the toast, and the severities towards the prisoners were in great measure increased or diminished, in proportion to the expectation of conquest. His very ostentatious proclamation was in the hand and mouth of most of the soldiery, especially the tories, and from it, their faith was raised to assurance.

I wish my countrymen in general could but have an idea of the assuming tyranny, and haughty, malevolent, and insolent behaviour of the enemy at that time; and from thence discern the intolerable calamities which this country have extricated themselves from by their public spiritedness and bravery.

The downfall of general Burgoyne, and surrender of his army,[52] dashed the aspiring hopes and expectations of the enemy, and brought low the imperious spirit of an opulent, puissant and haughty nation, and made the tories bite the ground with anguish, exalted the valour of the free-born sons of America, and raised their fame and that of their brave commanders to the clouds, and immortalized general Gates with laurels of eternal duration.

No sooner had the knowledge of this interesting and mighty event reached his Most Christian Majesty, who in Europe shines with a superior lustre in goodness, policy and arms, but the illustrious potentate, auspiciously influenced by Heaven to promote the reciprocal interest and happiness of the ancient kingdom of France, and the new and rising states of America, passed the great and decisive decree, that the United States of America, should be free and independent.

Vaunt no more Old England! consider you are but an island! and that your power has been continued longer than the exercise of your humanity. Order your broken and vanquished battalions to retire from America, the scene of your cruelties. Go home and repent in dust and sackcloth for your aggravated crimes. The cries of bereaved parents, widows, and orphans, reach the Heavens, and you are abominated by every friend to America. Take your friends the tories with you, and be gone, and drink deep of the cup of humiliation. Make peace with the princes of the house of Bourbon, for you are in no condition to wage war with them. Your veteran soldiers are fallen in America, and your glory is departed. Be quiet and pay your debts, especially for the hire of the Hessians. There is no other way for you

---

[52] Burgoyne surrendered to Gates at Saratoga on 17 October 1777.

LINK

"PROCLAMATION"

Burgoyne's "Proclamation" is an interesting document. John Burgoyne (1722–1792), whose nickname was "Gentleman Johnnie," was a wealthy aristocrat who, at various points in his career, served as a Member of Parliment, held the post of general in the British Army, and—one of his true passions—wrote plays for the theater. Several of his plays were quite successful in England and on the continent. He had been in Boston when the revolution began, but without a commission in the army. He went to England, procured a commission, and returned to command the army instructed to enter New York from Canada and link up with Sir William Howe's forces at Albany. The British hoped to hold a line along the Hudson River–Lake Champlain waterway that would effectively cut New England off from the rest of the American colonies (see map). Allen and Arnold knew what they were doing in 1775 when they captured Fort Ticonderoga!

Burgoyne's "Proclamation" is dramatic. The language and style are elevated. He imagines himself as a kind of director: "The forces entrusted to my command are designed to act in concert"; "I have but to give stretch to the Indian forces under my direction . . . to overtake the hardened enemies of Great Britain and America." It is a pompous, sententious document that was ruthlessly parodied at the time, even by Burgoyne's acquaintances. In the House of Commons, for example, Edmund Burke parodied Burgoyne's statement about his control of the Indian forces allied with him: "My gentle lions— my humane bears—my tenderhearted hyenas, go forth! But I exhort you, as you are Christians and members of civil society, to take care not to hurt any man, woman, or child." William Livingston, a congressman and governor of New Jersey—no friend of Burgoyne's— mocked his introductory paragraph:

> By John Burgoyne and Burgoyne, John, Esq.
> And graced with titles still more higher,
> For I'm Lieutenant-General, too,
> Of George's troops both red and blue,
> On this extensive continent;
> And of Queen Charlotte's regiment. . . .

> Directing too the fleet and troops
> From Canada as thick as hops;
> And all my titles to display,
> I'll end with thrice et cetera.

Burgoyne, as it turns out, could not control the Indian forces allied with him. Following his July 4 "Proclamation"—note that the date of the "Proclamation" is itself dramatic, claiming to counter the year-old Declaration of Independence—Burgoyne took Fort Ticonderoga from the Americans and then moved down to Lake George. At Fort Edward, Indian warriors seized a woman in her early twenties named Jane McCrea. They shot, scalped, mutilated and possibly tomahawked her, along with a family containing six children. Despite the fact that Jane McCrea was a Tory sympathizer, she became in the nineteenth century a folk heroine, the subject of countless poems and engravings.

to get into credit again but by reformation and plain honesty, which you have despised; for your power is by no means sufficient to support your vanity. I have had opportunity to see a great deal of it, and felt its severe effects, and learned lessons of wisdom and policy, when I wore your heavy irons, and bore your bitter revilings and reproaches. I have something of a smattering of philosophy, and understand human nature in all its stages tolerably well; am thoroughly acquainted with your national crimes, and assure you that they not only cry aloud for Heaven's vengeance, but excite mankind to rise up against you. Virtue, wisdom and policy, are in a national sense always connected with power, or in other words, power is their off-spring, and such power as is not directed by virtue, wisdom, and policy, never fails finally to destroy itself as yours has done,—It is so in the nature of things, and unfit it should be otherwise; for if it was not so, vanity, injustice, and oppression, might reign triumphant for ever. I know you have individuals, who still retain their virtue, and conse-quently their honour and humanity. Those I really pity, as they must more or less suffer in the calamity, in which the nation is plunged headlong; but as a nation I hate and despise you.

My affections are frenchified.—I glory in Louis the sixteenth, the generous and powerful ally of these states; am fond of a connection with so enterprizing, learned, polite, courteous, and commercial a nation, and am sure that I express the sentiments and feelings of all the friends to the present revolution. I begin to learn the French tongue, and recommend it to my countrymen before Hebrew, Greek or Latin, (provided but one of them only are to be attended to) for the trade and commerce of these states in future must inevitably shift its channel from England to France, Spain, and Portugal; and therefore the statesman, politician and merchant, need be acquainted with their several languages, particularly the French, which is much in vogue in most parts of Europe. Nothing could have served so effectually to illuminate, polish, and enrich these states as the present revolution, as well as preserve their liberty—Mankind are naturally too national, even to the degree of bigotry; and commercial intercourse with foreign nations has a great and necessary tendency, to improve mankind, and erase the superstition of the mind by acquainting them that human nature, policy and interest, are the same in all nations, and at the same time they are bartering commodities for the conveniences and happiness of each nation, they may reciprocally exchange such part of their customs and manners as may be beneficial, and learn to extend charity and good-will to the whole world of mankind.

I was confined in the provost-gaol at New York the twenty sixth day of August, and continued there to the third day of May, 1778, when I was taken out under guard, and conducted to a sloop in the harbour at New York, in which I was guarded to Staten Island, to general Campbell's quarters, where I was admitted to eat and drink with the general, and several other of the British field officers, and treated for two days in a polite manner. As I was drinking wine with them one evening, I made an observation on my transition from the provost-criminals to the company of gentlemen, adding that I was the same man still, and should give the British credit by him, (speaking to the general) for two days good usage.

The next day colonel Archibald Campbell (who was exchanged for me) came to this place, (conducted by Mr. Boudinot, the then American commissary of prisoners) and saluted me in a handsome manner, saying that he never was more glad to see any gentleman in his life, and I gave him to understand that I was equally glad to see him, and was apprehensive that it was from the same motive. The gentlemen present laughed at the fancy, and conjectured that sweet liberty was the foundation of our gladness; so we took a glass of wine together, and then I was accompanied by general Campbell, colonel

Campbell, Mr. Boudinot, and a number of British officers, to the boat, which was ready to sail to Elizabethtown-point. Mean while I entertained them with a rehearsal of the cruelties exercised towards our prisoners; and assured them that I should use my influence, that their prisoners should be treated in future in the same manner, as they should in future treat ours; that I thought it was right in such extreme cases, that their example should be applied to their own prisoners; then exchanged the decent ceremonies of compliment, and parted: I sailed to the point afore-said, and in a transport of joy, landed on liberty ground, and as I advanced into the country, received the acclamations of a grateful people.

I soon fell into company with col. Sheldon, (of the light horse) who in a polite and obliging manner, accompanied me to headquarters, Valley Forge, where I was courteously received by gen. Washington, with peculiar marks of his approbation and esteem, and was introduced to most of the generals and many of the principal officers of the army, who treated me with respect, and after having offered general Washington my further service, in behalf of my country, as soon as my health (which was very much impaired) would admit, and obtained his licence to return home, I took my leave of his excellency, and set out from Valley Forge with gen. Gates and his suite for Fish Kill, where we arrived the latter end of May. In this tour the general was pleased to treat me with the familiarity of a companion, and generosity of a lord, and to him I made known some striking circumstances which occurred in the course of my captivity.

I then bid farewel to my noble general and the gentlemen of his retinue, and set out for Bennington, the capital of the Green Mountain Boys, where I arrived the evening of the last day of May to their great surprise; for I was to them as one rose from the dead, and now both their joy and mine was complete. Three cannon were fired that evening, and next morning colonel Herrick gave orders, and fourteen more were discharged, welcoming me to Bennington, my usual place of abode; thirteen for the United States, and one for young Vermont.

After this ceremony was ended we moved the flowing bowl, and rural felicity, sweetened with friendship, glowed in each countenance, and with loyal healths to the rising States of America, concluded that evening, and with the same loyal spirit, I now conclude my narrative.

FINIS

Suggestions for Further Reading

Bailyn, Bernard. *The Ideological Origins of the American Revolution.* Cambridge, MA: Harvard Univ. Press, 1967.

Bellesiles, Michael A. *Revolutionary Outlaws: Ethan Allen and the Struggle for Independence on the Early American Frontier.* Charlottesville: Univ. Press of Virginia, 1993.

Hoyt, Edwin P. *The Damndest Yankees: Ethan Allen and his Clan.* Brattleboro, VT: The Stephen Greene Press, 1976.

Jellison, Charles A. *Ethan Allen: Frontier Rebel.* Syracuse: Syracuse Univ. Press, 1969.

McWilliams, John. "The Faces of Ethan Allen: 1760–1860." *The New England Quarterly* 49 (1976): 257–282.

Schama, Simon. *Citizens: A Chronicle of the French Revolution.* New York: Knopf, 1989.

Williams, Daniel. "Zealous in the Cause of Liberty: Self-Creation and Redemption in the Narrative of Ethan Allen." *Studies in Eighteenth-Century Culture* 19 (1989): 325–347.

Wills, Garry. *Inventing America: Jefferson's Declaration of Independence.* New York: Random House, 1978.

Wood, Gordon. *The Radicalism of the American Revolution.* New York: Knopf, 1991.